Penny Perspectives

Penny Perspectives:
Let Go of Happily Ever After & Invest in Happily Ever **NOW**!

Leslie Stein

First published by Dog Ear Publishing
4010 W. 86th Street, Ste H
Indianapolis, IN 46268
www.dogearpublishing.net

ISBN: 978-1-4575-1456-2

Dedication

To the stranger that dropped the $20 bill in a Washington, DC crosswalk on December 29, 2006. You changed my life.

If you've picked up a penny, dreamed a dream, or smiled at a stranger just because... this book is for you.

Penny Perspectives

I'd Like to Thank The Academy...

Why Acceptance Speeches Run Too Long & The People Giving Them Don't Care

If I have learned anything from picking up pennies over the last few years it is that each and every one of us has value. We may not always see it...but it is there. Sometimes it takes another to reflect our own value back to us. And sometimes it takes many of us coming together in collaboration to create the kind of value that can change lives.

I recognize that finding pennies on my own would not have gotten me very far. In fact, I probably would have stopped after the first year, content to satisfy my curiosity about how much money I could find in twelve months' time if I really paid attention.

But instead of being a lone penny finder, my enthusiasm & energy were met (and grown) by the people in my life who were willing to play with me and turn my curiosity into a calling. The people who time & time again reflected my own value back to me and allowed me to share with them the value they brought to my life.

The list is long and the reasons varied. And like each coin I find, every person has a special place in my heart for the role he or she played in making this project all that it could be. It is with huge appreciation and a heart overflowing with gratitude that I wish to thank those who have impacted me so greatly on this incredible journey.

To Illeny Maaza, my first official supporter. With the first penny you found & gave me, you changed this project from a solo endeavor to a collaboration. Without you, the grand total for the first 5 years would be a $252.36 less & this book 6 chapters shorter. In addition to being a penny-finding goddess, your work on the interior design of this book is a gift I will never forget. I cannot thank you enough for your support, your friendship, or your incredible generosity of spirit.

To Michele Bisceglie, the woman who saw an idea worth growing. Without your marketing genius & brilliant insight on our morning runs that first year, "The Penny Project" would never have existed. I would just be that weird girl picking up pennies and injured squirrels out of the gutter. Instead I became the weird girl who tried to save a squirrel once...but who has a really cool project people can get excited about.

To my family, quite possibly the most incredible people on the planet. There are not enough words to thank you for all you do for me. Not only do you collectively kick ass on penny-finding ($321.92 in the first 5 & ¼ years) but you inspire me daily and love me no matter what...truly priceless. To my dad, Jerry Stein, you are still the undisputed record holder for biggest single find ($250) as well as the best purveyor of penny poetry & "jazz hands" either side of the Mississippi. To my mom, Darlene Stein, I'm quite certain there would be no book without your belief in my ability to tell a story. Thank you for the countless brainstorming sessions, calls to get me back in my writer's vortex, & endless re-reads to make important decisions like should this be "a" penny or "the" penny? To my sister, Sarah Grecco, my life would lack a certain "je ne sais quoi" without you. You make me laugh & keep me sane. Hi. I'm in Delaware. I love you!!!

To Stephanie Giannori, for caring about every detail. You are a brilliant editor who polished my words to make me sound like the best version of myself. But even more important, you are a brilliant FRIEND who cares deeply about the people you love, willing to devour every detail of the stories of our lives. You are a tremendous listener, wickedly smart, and fun beyond measure. Thank you for your amazing friendship and for the clarity you brought to my writing.

To Alex Kube, for your patience and your art. You changed the cover design process from an overwhelming task I was terrified to begin to a joyful expression of what these stories mean to me. Your patience & coaching as the design unfolded made it a journey I was happy to be on. Thank you for stepping forward to say, "I can help you out!" when I needed it most!!

To my DC friends, creators of endless stories, pictures, poetry, & laughter about penny finding. Some of you mocked me endlessly at first (with very good reason) but always supported me...and eventually came around to see the magic of penny finding! There would have been no second year without that first year you helped me create. Hugs & high fives to Eric Hemati, Chad Rainey, Deborah Rainey, Amy Driscoll, Rick Yost, Heather King, April Canter, Marissa Gandelman, Lisa Lin, & Heather Robinson.

To Nicole Gianturco, my most fearless & fantastical supporter, not only in pennies but in life. I didn't know people could manifest money out of thin air until I met you. $10 bill...BAM! Your legendary penny finding stories are matched only by your incredible spirit. You are one of those people that I can't believe I was lucky enough to find...but then also know that it couldn't have been any other way. Thank you for being you.

To Sean Greystone, a seeker like none I've ever met. You taught me the true meaning and incredible power of pennies. You're amazing energy expands my mind & opens my heart every time we connect. Thank you for believing in me the way you do...the power of that is unmatched by anyone I've ever known.

To Ellie Willard, the only person EVER to find a half dollar coin. You are a magic maker. Not only with the half dollar but with so much more.

Thank you for your endless support, belief in me, & continued penny-picking-upping. A half dollar...it still leaves me speechless!

To Karina Bullard & the entire Kuhl-Bull clan (Terry, Jane, JJ, Allen, Parker & Tyler), for taking penny-finding to a whole new level!! You've been my best friend & second family ever since I can remember, bringing joy into my life in a million different ways. Your penny adventures are EPIC & only seem to get better the more fun you are having. Massive finds in amusement parks, piles of change at the bottom of a swimming pool, paper money at baseball games, $20 bills while on vacation, and of course...the infamous Penny Progressive Dinner! You bring fun to the world and most especially to my life. Thank you for the constant reminders to laugh & enjoy the ride!

To my Helo Hotties & Chinook-flying sisters, Misty Cornett Lever, Julia Brown Chandler, &

Jennifer Walsh Christenson, for some of my most memorable penny moments. From vacations in Hawaii to weddings in Washington, DC you're the kind of friends I wish everyone could have. You were there for me way before I discovered pennies...and I know you will be there for me long after I've forgotten about them.

To Tia Singh, bloggess extraordinaire, whose invitation to guest blog about what I learned from pennies made me realize these concepts are universal. We all forget the value of little moments and step over things that really matter. Your invitation made me stop stepping over the gift of these stories. Thank heavens for twitter (of all things?!) & a serendipitous trip to Vancouver leading me to a woman who truly sparkles...and shows others how they sparkle too!!

To Hugh O'Donnell, the most generous stranger I've ever met. Who brings $20+ in change to a first meeting...gift wrapped, nonetheless?! Your huge heart & unmatched generosity have blown me away over, and over, and over again. Thank you for moving from "stranger" to "friend" and for continuing to surprise & delight me with new ways to package pennies every time I see you!

To the Air Dragons, for listening and supporting. You were the first people to whom I read my stories aloud. These stories are from my life & more importantly, my heart, which makes sharing them scarier than you'd imagine. You not only provided a safe place to tell them (and massive loads of encouragement to take them to a bigger audience) but also shared yourselves through the creative ways you developed to contribute your pennies to the project (cookie-shaped change purses, fish-themed piggy banks, & $10 bills pulled from bras come to mind). You are amazing. Our journey together is a gift. These are my words.

To everyone who has shared time with me to help create the stories, moments, & happy memories held within this book, a HUGE thank you! Whether by name or by title, you're in these pages because you've impacted my life in a positive way...and I am grateful! Many thanks to Sara DeWitz, Niki Clark, Tim JohnPress, Ryan Moffett, Kate Kohler, Mike Nance, Bobby Miller, Brandie Fennell, Bill Olsen, Michael Wilkinson, Tierah Chorba, Melissa Sims, Laura Pohl, Amanda Coussoule, Frances Reimers, Erica Parkhurst, Jenn Schwartz, Rachel Kuypers, Sol & Rosann Stein, Dina Paxenos, Kay Marie Lavorini, & Kristen Sloan.

And for everyone who has ever given a penny, shared an idea, or celebrated a crazy find with me...I thank you too. Your proverbial "2 cents" is much appreciated and was often the fuel that kept me going.

Each moment has been wonderful...but it is the sum total of all the generosity I've encountered that completely blows my mind. The world is a wonderful place and I feel blessed to have seen it through such an incredible lens.

The next time you find a penny, may you be reminded of the joy, laughter, & abundance available to you right now & in every moment!

And that's my 2 cents. Happy reading!

"Your life does not get better by chance, it gets better by CHANGE."
--Jim Rohn

How I Found Happiness – For Just Pennies A Day!

Why The Following Story is Largely Responsible For The Book You Are Now Holding

S ome time ago, my friend and colleague, Coach Tia, asked me to write my penny story as a guest blogger on her Web site, a blog that focuses on living from a place of inspiration and creating the life you want. As I am always happy when someone wants to hear about pennies, I gladly agreed to her request.

When Tia posted my blog on her Web site, I was so overwhelmed with the notes and words of encouragement I received from her readers — as well as my own friends who visited her Web site to read it — that I decided to write more of my penny stories.

And so, I embarked on this new adventure. The journey was a quick one — I wrote the book in 34 days, which is a whole story in itself! I think it was easy because writing about the lessons I've learned, and am continuing to learn, from pennies makes me smile and warms my heart. And who doesn't want to feel that way?

So for 34 days, I wrote diligently to create a series of stories that are intended to remind us of things we already know, to make us laugh, and to help us re-engage after a hard day by asking ourselves, *"Do I take advantage of all the opportunities for happiness in my life?"*

This book is for those who've ever picked up a penny and smiled because, hey, it's free money! It's also for those who pass up the pennies they see because, well, it's just a penny.

Whichever camp you're in, I hope that after reading my story, you will look at pennies a little differently the next time you find one on the street. If you let them, pennies may just be the gateway into noticing the other things in your life that could bring you great happiness!

The Original Penny Post

I've learned an incredible amount in the last 3 years.

There have been lots of reasons for this — classes I've attended, people I've met, the places I've traveled, the challenging work I pushed myself to take on, etc. But of all the places I visited and all the things I experienced, I have to admit that the largest part of my learning came from a place I never expected.

Most of what I've learned in the last three years,
I learned from pennies.

Yep, pennies — those little 1-cent jobbers most people ignore without a second look.

You're probably wondering, "What could you have possibly learned from a penny?!"

Believe it or not, the answer is that I've picked up some pretty huge life lessons. I guess I should attempt to explain myself.

Ok, where do I begin? I guess it all started on December 29, 2006, when I randomly found a $20 bill in the crosswalk on my way home from work. I'm not usually one for New Year's resolutions, but this $20 bill got me thinking (after I finished my happy dance and spent the money on a good pedicure) about the way we view money in today's world.

I mean, really, were people just tossing $20s in the street? I think I may have pinpointed the source of our economic woes!

Long story short, I decided to start picking up all the change I found in 2007 to see how much I'd end up with by the end of the year. So I started picking up pennies, or really any money I found on the ground, but mostly pennies.

I was pretty shocked at how much I was finding.

- By June 2007 I had about $15 and a handful of friends bringing me their pennies.
- By September 2007 I had started a blog about my money-finding adventures, and had been filmed for a short movie about pennies.
- By the end of the year, my little band of change collectors and I had amassed over $85 in total.

Not bad.

All the while this "Penny Project" was going on, I was having a series of meltdowns about why my life wasn't turning out to be a "10." I wanted to be happy like everyone else.

Why couldn't I find someone to date in DC? Why had I been a bridesmaid seven times and never a bride? Why, why, why, WHY?!

I was having these meltdowns via telephone with my mom (who also happens to be one of my closest friends) on a routine basis. Every time I called, I kept asking her why my life wasn't a 10.

Finally, one day, she said, *"Are you so sure it's not?"*

Um, yeah…I think I'd know if my life was a 10. So I asked her to clarify what I thought to be a very un-smart reply to my serious woes.

Her theory was that I had a lot of good days. She said, "Let's call these days '7s', and every once in awhile, you have a REALLY good day, which we'll call '10s.'" It turns out that my mom could list off several of these days without trying too hard. Like, for example, the day a friend of mine took me to The Grammy Awards in California. It was hard not to call that day a 10, even when I was pouting on the phone with my mom about my lackluster life.

She said that maybe all I needed was a series of 7s and a 10 every now and then, for my life to be a 10.

Huh?!

I was a language major and not always the best with numbers, so I had no idea what kind of "new math" gave my mom the idea that $7+7+7=10$.

In short, I wasn't buying what she was selling.

Then one day, on my way home, I found a $5 bill on the street. I was so excited I could barely contain myself. I'm pretty sure I screamed and completely freaked out the lady walking behind me.

I know $5 doesn't sound like much, but pick up grimy pennies out of the gutter for a few months and, trust me, you'll have a whole new appreciation for a fiver!

So I got home and added my $5 to the money-finding spreadsheet I used to track my "successes" and saw that I had broken the $20-mark for the year. I had been secretly challenging myself to see if that would happen. Imagine the feeling I had when I realized that with several months left in the year, I had already exceeded my $20 goal, and bested the $20 find that started this whole project.

It was a nice moment.

Over the next few days on my walks to work, which were more than 2-miles each way (aka, lots of time to think and scan the sidewalk for pennies), I compared my life to the Penny Project.

I started thinking about my mom's comments and equated my findings to the scale we'd been talking about.

- Finding paper money of any kind — that is definitely a 10, or what I would call a "peak experience." Major excitement involved, possibly some screaming.
- Finding a quarter — gotta give that a 9. That's 25 pennies. All at once. Definitely a week-maker.
- Nickels and dimes — those are 8s. Seeing silver definitely makes me smile. It's not a huge deal, but damn, it's exciting to see a shiny thing on the sidewalk and realize it's more than 1 cent!
- Finally, our friend the penny comes in at a 7. You can't buy anything with it. Most people get so annoyed with them that they just leave them on the sidewalk if they drop one.

But since starting my project, I'd grown to appreciate the little buggers and definitely got a warm fuzzy feeling whenever I found one.

It wasn't enough to make me think that finding one — or several, as was typically the case during my walk to and from work — made it a red letter day. But each one definitely made me smile and think of the money tracking spreadsheet and my friends who were also looking for pennies on my behalf. By then, my list of penny contributors was up to 30 or 40 people — in less than one year!

As the year came to a close, I tallied up all the pennies and other money that my contributors and I had found. In 2007, I found a total of $32.76. And with all the money my friends found and contributed, the total was up to $85.56. Not bad for abandoned coins and the occasional paper currency.

As I looked at the totals, I thought back to my mom's "new math" and heard her saying, "Maybe 7+7+7=10." Was it possible she was right?!

After a year of picking up these grubby, little coins, I could see that the majority of what I'd found had been pennies. Sure, there were a few quarters and dimes (and that very exciting $5 bill) in the total, but mostly I'd accumulated a whole bunch of "7s."

And when it was all said and done, they added up to MORE than my original $20 find, which I thought of as a "10." Crap! I love my mom, but I really hate having to call her and tell her she was right.

So here's what I've concluded from this rather ridiculous experience. Happiness is there, you just have to **see** it.

Figure out what the 7's are in your life!

Most people don't need help with the 10s — marriage, birth of a child, graduation, promotions, and all the other good stuff we celebrate with parties. But few of us ever consider the 7s.

When I started to really pay attention to those 7 days, I found there were a lot more than I had realized. And most of those days were made up of small, silly things.

Like the fact I totally love getting the mail. Don't know why, I just always have. Even if it's just junk mail or the mailbox is empty, there's that moment of anticipation before I open the mailbox where I think that maybe, just maybe, today's the day I get something really, really good!

I also rate as 7's:

- a good cup of coffee
- sleeping in
- wearing my pink galoshes in the rain
- my cats purring

I could go on and on, but the point isn't to list all my 7s, it's to inspire other people to think about theirs.

What are your life's pennies?

Do you take stock of them and put them in your emotional piggy bank, or just overlook them as unimportant because, really, what's a penny gonna get you?

As silly as finding happiness in pennies sounds, it really has made a huge impact on my life. And in fact, it's made an impact on some other lives as well.

Since starting this project, hundreds of people have donated money they found, opened their wallets, written me checks, or just emptied their pockets and handed over the loose change rattling around.

When we hit the $500 mark early in the third year of the project, we donated the money to the first annual Young Women's National Conference, which focused on promoting self-esteem for young girls 14-17 years old. All those pennies paid for the financial literacy panel at the event!

Of course, I still don't have life completely figured out. There are still tearful calls to my mom wondering why I've now been a bridesmaid 9 times and am on deck for number 10.

But the tears don't last as long because I can look around at my warm cup of coffee, the keys to my mailbox, my purring cats, and all my pennies to see that even without having EVERYTHING I want, my life really IS a 10 after all!

Baby Steps

Why Thinking Too Far Ahead Doesn't Only Keep You From Crossing The Finish Line… It Keeps You From Stepping Up To The Start Line

B esides being a super-cool, high-speed, US Army helicopter pilot in 1999, I also sold Mary Kay cosmetics. Try and make those two things make sense in your Christmas letter!

"Defending Freedom & Helping You Moisturize"
or
"Yes I'm a Bad Ass… But My Lips Are Always Glossy"

The possibilities were endless.

Although my stint in cosmetic sales was short-lived, I learned some valuable life lessons from my Mary Kay sisters! During my six months with the company, I had the good fortune of attending a few regional meetings and hearing some really great speakers.

One piece of advice has stuck with me above all the rest from that period of my life. It came from a class on business building, in which the speaker said, "If you waited to leave your house until every light between home and your final destination was green…you'd never get out the front door!"

Wow! That analogy was so obvious but so true! How many times had I delayed doing something until all the conditions were "perfect", only to learn that moment of perfection never came?

The speaker went on to tell us that any worthwhile effort would have bumps in the road. From minor inconveniences (yellow lights) to big setbacks (red lights), it is rare that a journey goes exactly as planned.

It was like she was giving us all permission to do the best job we could and not worry about making mistakes. In fact, she told us about some of the mistakes on her own journey — which was overall a hugely successful one — further demonstrating that yellow and red lights are OK. What a refreshing angle!

But what happens when you haven't yet identified the destination? Should you still leave the house? I was all for a few yellow and red lights, but what about driving around aimlessly and wasting gas?

This question had been on my mind when two friends asked me to join them for a weekend jog. Niki was training for a marathon and needed moral support for her long runs. I needed to figure out what the heck life path I was on while catching up with my friends and getting a little exercise.

When we got to the trail and were ready to start running, Niki informed us that she was planning to run seven miles that day.

SEVEN MILES?! I don't even drive that far on a regular basis. "Um, you didn't expect us to run all of that with you, did you?"

"Well, I was thinking we could do the first five with her," said our other friend Sara.

I still wasn't on board.

"People! I love ya'll, but there is no way this body is running seven miles. Or five. I was thinking like… three. And I planned to walk a fair amount of that. How about we run half a mile together and see how we feel after that?"

They both agreed (since they knew all I'd commit to was half a mile) and off we went.

When we hit the first half-mile marker we were deep in conversation about boys and barely noticed we'd been running at all.

"Another half?" they asked me.

"Yeah, I'm good."

The same thing happened at the 1-mile marker. Three girls clearly have a lot to talk about when it comes to boys. "Another half?"

"Ok," I replied.

And so on. And so on.

This pattern repeated until we hit the 4-mile marker, at which point we took a brief walk break before starting to run again.

In the end, I was feeling pretty good and ran the last mile at a faster pace, which resulted in my finishing first and waiting for the girls by the car. Isn't it funny that the biggest whiner, who was sooooo certain she couldn't run 5 miles, let alone 7, ended up finishing before everyone else?

Looking back, the reason I was able to run 7 miles was because I didn't have to commit to running 7 miles. All I had to do was commit to a series of half-mile increments and reevaluate how I felt when each one was finished. That was something I was willing to sign up for.

Oddly enough, The Penny Project unfolded in much the same way. It started out of sheer curiosity to see how much money I could find on the ground in a year. All I was committing myself to was picking up a few pennies. I was willing to do that.

If someone had said to me on January 1, 2007:

"Ok, Leslie, what we need you to do over the next three years is start a blog, convince hundreds of strangers to give you money, raise $500 for charity, find a way to be part of a documentary about pennies, get people excited about finding pennies, find people to post your story on their Web sites, and then write a book about it all."

I would have said, "Um, YOU'RE crazy. Thanks, but no thanks."

I guess it's a good thing that all I had to commit to was finding one penny at a time.

Lesson

Although goals and long term visions are important, don't get so caught up in all the details that you never take the first step. And whatever you do, don't wait for all the lights to turn green before you get moving!

I promise you that when I started collecting pennies I had no earthly idea what I was getting myself into. How could I have possibly predicted that grown adults would get such joy in finding pennies? That they would encourage me to start a blog about it or want to share their own lessons learned?

And could I have EVER dreamed up that a film crew would find my blog and ask me to be one of their "pro-penny" subjects for a documentary about "the changing face of change?" Could YOU have dreamed that up? When does that ever happen?

My point is this: do things you enjoy, things that GIVE you energy. When you do — no matter how silly or seemingly crazy they are-- you'll tap into a level of curiosity, engagement, and (dare I say it) FUN that is almost impossible to ignore.

When that happens, the logical next step always presents itself, and before you know it, you've not only left the start line, but you're well on your way to crossing the finish line. Or better yet, you might realize you don't care about the finish line at all because each step of the journey is so much darn fun, and every red light just gives you a chance to look around and enjoy how far you've come!

What are your 2 cents?

- What are the yellow and red lights that keep you from "leaving the house?"
- What activities do you love so much that you'd do them even if there was no "finish line" or "final destination?"
- How can you integrate more of those activities into your life to see where they might take you?

Signs
Why The Universe May Be Talking To You
But You're Just Not Listening

I was never one who used to believe in signs. I didn't think God was talking to me through a billboard or the Universe was trying to tell me something in my fortune cookie. Sure, there might have been the occasional coincidence that was just a little hard to ignore, but I always figured that kind of stuff only happened to special people. I didn't think that meant me.

But the more I study various spiritual teachers and religions, the more I'm convinced that God, the Universe, source energy, or whatever you choose to call it, talks to people in ways that make sense to them. (Or in my case cents).

Some people channel spirits. Others have amazing abilities and talents. I find pennies.

I'm not even sure what that means. Did the Universe think I was money hungry and would only be able to talk to me in dollars and cents? After all, it took a $20 bill for me to notice that there even WAS money on the ground anywhere. I'd never paid attention to stuff like that before.

Anyhow, as I started finding pennies more and more regularly, I started noticing some patterns.

For instance, I almost always find money when I'm going to the gym or go running. I never find money when I'm sitting on my couch eating a pint of Ben & Jerry's. Not that I think the Universe is claiming one of these activities is better than the other, but I do think I'm on the life path I want to lead when I'm being healthy rather than when I'm sucking back 1500 calories of Chunky Monkey. And I think the Universe is helping me to confirm that.

I also notice that when I'm with people who accept or even encourage my crazy penny finding ways, I find lots of money. And often, they find money, too, and hand it right to me!

When I'm with people who judge me and tell me I'm a nutcase, I don't find many pennies. Perhaps the Universe is helping me learn not to waste my time on people who don't love me as I am.

The point is I've begun to see the pennies as somewhat of a sign I'm on the right track. Sometimes I even ask for one. "Universe, am I really where I need to be right now? If so, give me a sign." Within minutes, I'll either find a penny or a reason to change course.

The best instance of this occurred when I was in a bit of flux about the next step I needed to take for my future.

I was in the middle of a particularly intense series of jobs with five different clients, all of whom were wonderful, but some of them were extremely demanding. On top of that, I had an impending 4-day visit with the guy I was dating long distance, my mom was in town for a week helping me with business planning, my sister needed my help with wedding dress shopping (which required driving back and forth to her house an hour away), and I was meeting with my good friend and silent business partner, Kate, about my next steps for a venture she was helping to support financially.

I didn't have time to breathe let alone decide if I was "on the right path."

On top of all this activity, I'd also committed several thousand dollars of my own money to pay for a leadership course I desperately wanted to attend. This was the first big investment in my own self-education I'd ever made and it was a bit scary.

Leadership fascinates me and I was hoping this course would help me figure out where I wanted to go as a leader, to discover my personal mission both in my own life and the lives of others as well as in and my own business .

No pressure.

One weekend, smack dab in the middle of my crazy schedule, the exhaustion started to set in.

I'd returned from visiting the guy I was seeing and wasn't exactly sure where (if anywhere at all) our relationship was going. I'd been home a whopping 9 hours when I had to get in the car to go meet my sister and mom at a bridal shop to watch my sister try on dresses. She not only found one in record time, but also for a record 70% off discounted price — talk about saving a few pennies!

As we headed back to my sister's house for dinner, I had a bit of a meltdown with my mom in the car. I told her I was sure I wanted teamwork in my life, but I had somehow managed to have both a personal and professional life devoid of any. Single at the age of 34 and working as a contract consultant, I didn't know where to find my "team."

After a teary meal and lots of hugs from my supportive family, I got in the car and headed to my next stop — late night walk with Kate.

It was a crisp fall night, so we bundled up and took a stroll around the neighborhood. Kate was recovering from a 100-mile Trans-Rockies road race, which meant a well deserved rest from working out too hard. But we both like to be active, so chatting over a walk was perfect.

When we got back to her place, we continued talking and sat on her living room floor with two cups of hot tea. She'd just moved in and didn't have any living room furniture yet. I personally found sitting on the floor with our tea to be charming and felt it was quite special to be one of her first guests. Real friends don't mind sitting on the floor before the furniture arrives!

Kate is a wonderful mentor, not to mention one of the smartest people I know. When I told her I'd committed to paying my own way to the leadership course, she said she was very proud of me. She thought it was a big deal that this was the first education I would be paying for myself. It would be an investment in my own growth.

I had never thought of it that way, but appreciated her support and enthusiasm for my decision.

While I was there, she also loaned me a book she'd used while getting her MBA at Harvard (this was after her graduation from West Point, which is where I met her; I told you she was one of the smartest people I know!). The book was called "True North: Discover Your Authentic Leadership." It was a signed copy written by one of her professors at Harvard.

She said it had been a great help to her and thought I might benefit from reading it before embarking on my own study of leadership.

By this time, it had started getting late and I decided I'd better be on my way. I hugged Kate and thanked her for the friendship and advice. And for allowing me to be one of her first guests!

My general penny-finding-guideline at the time (a mini goal for how many pennies I like to find per day) was 15. I'd found 13 already that day and was pretty happy with that. As I left Kate's place and walked back to my car, I found a 14th penny. I was one penny away from my daily goal.

I looked to see if maybe there was another one nearby. No luck.

Happy with my 14 pennies, I hopped in the car and drove home.

Upon my arrival at home-sweet-home, I immediately donned my PJs and hopped into bed. I had brought "True North" with me and thought I'd flip through a few pages to see if it would be the next book I'd tackle, or if it might fall a little lower in my pile.

I'd read a particularly annoying leadership book recently and actually had to put it down half way through. I'd never done that with a book before. I decided then and there, life was too short to read books that sucked.

So, I settled into my bed to peruse the intro of "True North" to see if it piqued my interest. I was sure Kate wouldn't lead me astray, but I wanted to make sure it spoke to me.

I opened up the book to the dedication. I occasionally like to read dedications and see who inspired the author. In this case, I figured it might be a clue as to the kind of person the author was.

I stared down at the page and, for a second, thought someone was pulling my leg. The dedication read:

This book is dedicated to my wife, Penny.

There was my 15th penny of the day! I guess that's as good a sign as any that this was definitely the next book I was meant to read!

And so, I've learned to appreciate the signs in my life. I've heard people out there say the Universe whispers to you and if you don't listen, it might yell. And if that doesn't work, sometimes it just has to smack you upside the head. I think a penny is a pretty nice way of letting me know I'm on the right path. Certainly better than a smack upside the head!

Better yet, the pennies have come with some great lessons that I really wasn't expecting to learn. I know it sounds silly, but we can't always choose our teachers, can we? And who knows how many signs I passed before I started listening? Maybe some of the frustrations and heartbreaks could have been avoided if I'd only seen the signs!

Lesson

The Universe speaks to us in ways we're likely to hear. I'm not sure why pennies have been the vehicle of my greatest learning. Apparently, I'm either money hungry or a closet numismatist.

Whatever the reason, I am thankful I was open to the lessons. Although, I admit, it didn't start out that way. For over a year, I resisted my mom's theory that $7+7+7=10$ (if you need a reminder of how this equation works, see the introduction!). And yet, the pennies kept coming. I collected over $32 worth that first year, enough to show me that maybe her theory was right and that maybe there were other lessons to learn.

Look around in your life and find the things that keep popping up. The inexplicable coincidences or the funny instances you laugh about and share with others. It's these times when you're amazed or amused that you're most open to learning. Your resistance is gone and you're caught up in a moment of "I wonder… "

What are your 2 cents?

- Take a moment to look back and see if there are any coincidences that keep popping up. Do you think there could be a message there from the Universe?
- When is your resistance gone?
- When do you find yourself most amazed or amused?
- What might your unlikely teacher be?

Silver Linings & Positive Attitudes

Why You Might As Well Make The Best of a Bad Situation Because If You Don't, You'll Have a Bad Situation AND A Bad Attitude

Hang with me. This story meanders a bit, but so do our days sometimes, don't they? We have the intention to go straight from A to B, and then life happens. We depart A and end up hitting C & D & E… and maybe even F…before we finally make it to our final destination. But when we look back, we realize that A to B wouldn't have served us nearly as well as the meandering journey we ended up taking.

Ah, now what to say about the topic of silver linings. Here goes.

They exist. Try to find them. Thank you for reading.

You probably want a little more than that, eh?

Fair enough. This is one of those pieces of advice you've probably heard a million times in a million different ways. But perhaps the penny perspective on silver (or sometimes copper) linings will be the one that sticks with you. It's worth a shot!

The thing with silver linings is that you're no worse off if you can't find one, so you're not losing anything by looking. In fact, sometimes the mere act of trying to find a silver lining makes the situation better.

I experienced a prime example of this one year at Christmas.

When I decided to write this book, I thought it would be fun to write it the last 34 days of my 34th year. My mom had mentioned to me that a friend of hers wrote his book in 35 days — that's what really started it all. Being the competitive type, I took the bait and declared the 34-day writing challenge to be on.

The challenge was in the fact that my birthday is on January 14. If you count backwards 34 days from my birthday, you will conveniently notice that my writing challenge fell right in the middle of the holidays. So, I started writing this book on December 11. My routine lasted all of 5 days before my parents came to town for the holidays for just shy of two weeks. This meant driving to the airport, trips to the grocery store (to stock my normally sad looking fridge), and a 5-day stay out in the 'burbs' with my sister and her fiancé for our annual Christmas gift-giving bonanza.

Don't get me wrong, I'm one of those people who won the family lottery. I'm the only 34-year old I know who still vacations with her parents. I'm not even forced or shamed into it. I just like it. They're super-fun people (must be where I get it!).

But no matter how much you love your family, having them drop into your life during the middle of a busy period messes with your routine and can be a bit stressful. This is especially true when you have only one real bedroom and give it to your parents, relegating yourself to couch status for six nights. Add to that my engrained sense of good hostess duties, and I ended up tucking everyone in at day's end and writing stories from 1-3 a.m. from my couch/bed.

Then it was off to my sister's (where I was upgraded to a futon and my own room) for five more days of family fun. I was actually quite prolific during this period considering all that was going on. I cranked out at least one story each night, which was pretty darn productive given the circumstances!

When the holidays were over and everyone had gone back to their respective homes, I was really looking forward to getting back to some kind of routine (even if only for a couple days before leaving for my New Year's Eve trip).

I said good-bye, packed up the car, and got on the road. That lasted a whole 4 minutes before my car started shaking violently. It had taken me a few tries to get it started, so I thought it was just sluggish from sitting for five days in a snow drift.

Nope. Turns out I had a flat tire. Thankfully, my GPS guided me to a nearby tire servicing place to see if I could get some help. I knew it wasn't great to drive on a flat, but it was more appealing than having to ask my brother-in-law for assistance in the rain/snow. He later told me I was selfish for not asking for his help as I had deprived him of the chance to hold the incident over my head for years to come. At least I know that next time he's willing to rescue me if he can hold it over my head for the next several decades!

So there I was, tired, wet, with my trunk filled to the gills with presents and suitcases, and not exactly thrilled that I was about to plunk down God-only-knows-how-much to get this tire fixed.

My car limped into the parking lot and I parked it in the first somewhat clear space I could find. Not a parking space… just space.

I got out of the car and locked it behind me. Not that I thought anyone was after my 1997 Geo Prizm, but rather all my presents in the trunk! I didn't need missing iPod speakers added to my list of reasons to be annoyed at the moment.

I could feel my "grumpy pants" tightening around my waist as I walked towards the door to the office. Just as I was about to open the door, I turned and looked at the parking space another customer had just backed out of.

There, looking me in the face was a quarter. A QUARTER!

I thought maybe it was a gum wrapper and the Universe was mocking me (and my flat tire). But no, it was an actual quarter, sitting there as if it was waiting for me to find it.

Having just written the chapter about signs, I took this as a big one that I'd ended up in just the right place and was exactly where I needed to be for that moment in time. On this gray, rainy, tire-destroying day, here was my own personal silver lining. It's really hard not to smile when something like that happens.

Despite the situation, I found my mood turning around on the spot. I walked into the shop and explained what had happened. They checked out the tire rim while I entertained myself in the grocery store across the parking lot (where I found some excellent gifts for the people I was going to visit for New Year's Eve AND two more quarters).

When I got back to the tire shop, they told me I had indeed destroyed the rim and they had no replacement. Well, at least' I'd found three quarters while I was waiting.

The rest of the day ended up being a comedy of errors that led to wrong turns and unintended stops. On my way out of town I had a few errands to run. As I left the tire place, I drove past a Good Year store. Surely THEY would have what I needed.

Turns out they didn't, but the guy who spoke with me told me how to find deeply discounted auto parts online. I'd been thinking about writing a book about reward points, bargains, and doing things on the cheap, and here was this guy giving me chapter one. Hysterical!

When I left that location, I entered Wal-Mart into my GPS so I could pick up a shirt I wanted. Instead of taking me to a Wal-Mart, it took me to a DSW shoe store. I was in the mood to follow signs and I thought that if the Universe wanted to deliver me to a DSW (which is my favorite shoe store of all time), the least I could do was go in and look around. For the Universe, you know.

Four pairs of shoes later, I re-entered Wal-Mart in my GPS and crossed my fingers for better luck. This time I was successful! Not only did I find the shirt I was looking for, but I also grabbed three adorable dresses for $11 each. Score! Apparently chapter two in my next book will be about finding deals wherever your GPS takes you!

I left the store ecstatic about my finds and the positive turnaround that my day had taken. Not to mention that The Penny Project also scored big — I'd found a total of 80¢ (Wal-Mart yielded five pennies).

On the way back to my car, I called my sister to let her know I had gotten held up and wouldn't be back in the city for another hour. She'd planned to stop by after an appointment she had downtown, so I told her she could let herself into my apartment if she wanted to. Even though we'd just spent five days together, we're always up for a sister date and I was bummed I might miss her.

When I got to my car, I put my bag in the trunk and made a phone call. As I was chatting with my friend, a crazed-psychopath scared the daylights out of me by pounding on my passenger side window.

After I got my heart out of my throat and gathered my wits about me, I looked up to realize the crazed psychopath was my SISTER!! Apparently, she'd already returned from the city and was running errands herself. As she looked for an empty spot in the over-crowded Wal-mart parking lot, she saw my car and wondered to herself, "Who the hell else drives a 1997 Apricot Ice Geo Prizm?" When she realized it was me, she could barely believe it and had to sneak up to take a peak and make sure.

Sure, she nearly made me pee my pants, but at least I got to show her my new shoes and dresses! It was actually a really funny moment.

After our Wal-Mart fashionista trunk-show, I got back in my car and drove (slowly, on my spare) back home. I thought about all that had happened and how that quarter had totally turned my mood around. It had turned out to be a really fun day, although it was not at all what I was expecting.

I'd had a series of "tiki tours" as my friend Sara likes to call them (she doesn't believe in being lost, her motto is that we're always on a "tiki tour," which sounds so much more adventurous and cool than, "I have no idea where we are."). Besides, are we ever REALLY lost, or are we just living an experience we hadn't planned? Each stop I'd made that afternoon was fun and informative, and motivated me to get home and write about them. I eventually accomplished the tasks on my "to do" list, but I also got to have a memorable adventure along the way!

But I wonder what my attitude would have been had I not had the joy of finding that first quarter to help me turn my sour mood around? Once again, The Penny Project saved the day and provided me with a silver lining to what could have gone down as a no-good-horrible-very-bad-day.

Lesson

When you find yourself in a bad situation, look around to see what the good parts might be. I guarantee there are some. Whether you'll acknowledge them is a whole different question!

Once you find the silver lining of a situation, hold onto it and find the tangential things that make you happy. In my case, one quarter led to wandering around a grocery store because I decided that would be more fun than sitting in an office and waiting around. The wandering led to finding a few fun gifts, which led to the checkout lanes where I found two more quarters, and so on, and so on…

No matter what you find yourself doing, that's the situation you're in. My tire wasn't getting any less flat whether I was in a good mood or a bad mood. So I had to ask myself…do I want to have a flat tire AND be miserable all day? Or would I rather let the experts worry about the flat tire and figure out how to enjoy this pit stop on my way home? The only choice I had was my attitude.

Given the choice, I'd take a bad situation with a good attitude over a good situation with a bad attitude every time. Mostly because it always seems the situation usually turns around to match your attitude when you give it a fighting chance.

What are your 2 cents?

- When things don't go as you'd planned what choice of attitude do YOU make?
- How does your choice of attitude make the situation better?
- Think back to a situation that seemed bad at first, but then quickly turned into something positive later simply because you refused to think negatively. What helped you find the silver lining in that case?
- Where else in your life might you start looking for silver linings?

Mistakes

Why Mistakes, Like Pennies, Add Value To Your Life

Ah, mistakes. No matter how hard you try to avoid them, they're going to happen. Of course, most of the time, they're not the life shattering events we've made them out to be in our heads.

In fact, without making mistakes we would miss out on learning valuable lessons or information we didn't know was out there!

This is what happened to me about a month prior to beginning the journey of writing this book.

I had met a really cool coach on, of all places, Twitter! Being new to coaching and new to Twitter, I was excited to connect with such an interesting woman.

Tia is a real go-getter and someone I really loved following online. I ended up joining a call she hosted about procrastination, which was fascinating and helpful. It completely reframed the way I look at doing things on my own timeline (i.e., usually there's a REASON we put things off, and it's not because we're lazy, which is what we often tell ourselves in our heads!).

We "tweeted" back and forth for a few months and I found her to have such a great outlook on life. A true teacher — and in the last place I'd have expected to find one!

While this was going on, I was planning a trip to Vancouver with a good friend of mine. I tweeted that I was excited about the trip and Tia wrote back, "I live in Vancouver…we should meet up!"

I thought this was a fabulous idea! I figured even if my friend wasn't up for meeting strangers in cafes, she could entertain herself while Tia and I chatted for a few hours.

Soon enough the time for the trip was upon us and my friend Stephanie and I flew to Vancouver. The trip was amazing! Our hotel was in a perfect location with a breathtaking view. We had three excursions planned, and our hotel concierge said we couldn't have picked better ones if we'd tried. We even had a few unplanned days to take advantage of last minute things that we discovered once we arrived.

At the end of one lazy day of strolling around Vancouver's well known Stanley Park, we headed downtown to meet up with Tia for coffee. Steph didn't mind tagging along, so we wandered into town together.

We met up easily (or as easily as two people can while trying to find someone they've only seen on a small thumbnail photo on Twitter) and headed to a nearby coffee shop. Me being me, I found 16 cents on the floor by the register. I excitedly picked them up while Stephanie shook her head and Tia looked on a bit puzzled.

Over the course of the next several hours — boy did all three of us hit it off! — we talked about all sorts of things, including the pennies. Tia loved the story and asked if I'd be interested in writing a guest post for her blog.

Wow…I never thought my penny story would be all that interesting to an audience beyond the friends and family who bring me their pennies. The whole idea of reaching other people was exciting! Who knew picking up pennies in that coffee shop would lead to an opportunity to share my story?!

I agreed to guest blog and set a deadline to turn in my piece. This coffee date was turning out even cooler than I could have imagined!

With our drinks long gone and the sun past set, Steph and I said goodbye to Tia and headed back to the hotel. It had been a somewhat magical afternoon in the way we all clicked and the conversation flowed. And of course, the opportunity to write for Tia's blog was very exciting for me!

The rest of the vacation was fantastic, but then it was back to real life. The following month was hectic with work and friends coming to visit. Then, finally, I got to sit down and write the penny story for Tia's blog. It was much easier to write than I had expected. Like the conversation that afternoon in the coffee shop, it just seemed to flow.

I sent it to Tia and before I knew it, my piece was posted on her site for all to see. There was a great string of comments and conversation about the piece — very motivating to me as a writer! In fact, that blog entry became the forward to this book.

Well, like one is apt to do when filled with excitement about something, I spread the word about my blog post. I talked about it, tweeted about it, posted a link on my Facebook page about it…and on, and on, and on.

When another colleague of mine (a coach I'd met in one of my classes) asked if she could post my story on her blog, I was beyond excited. Really?! ANOTHER opportunity to share my love of pennies and the life lessons they'd taught me?! This was FANTASTIC!

I sent her the file, she posted the story, and again I tweeted, Facebooked, and spread the word.

A day later, I got a message from Tia. Always happy to hear from her, I opened it with excitement to see what she was up to.

Congrats on your 2nd guest post! How Awesome!!!!

I just remembered though, that when I did something similar (i.e., posted identical content on 2 websites), the guy whose blog I posted on told me it negatively affected his and my website rankings by creating a duplicate content issue.

100% same content on 2 different websites should be avoided as it results in a slap on the wrist and lowered traffic /credibility. So if you are going to use the exact same article on other sites, pretty please could you change it around somewhat? :)

I had no idea about all this until my friend told me, so I'm being careful now. Not to take away from your wonderful writing and guest posting — of course your story is awesome and worth telling over and over! xoxoxo MWah!

Wow…not exactly the message I was hoping for. I felt genuinely awful that I might have not only damaged Tia's web traffic and credibility, but my other friend's website as well.

What a numbskull!

I immediately wrote back, apologizing for my mistake. Tia's response was supportive and even encouraged me to continue writing. Pretty amazing considering I'd just inadvertently screwed up her web-world!

I only learned about this a few weeks ago myself, so don't sweat it sista. ;) Good to have people who know this stuff around me so I don't wonder what happened later on, hehe. Don't think it has affected website rankings yet, but it may down the line when spiders crawl for content. Gotta revamp the website anyhoo, so I'm not obsessed about numbers at the moment, but handy tip to know, hey! Thanks muchos for talking about me to your friends, really truly appreciate your support, xoxo. And yes, write ON!!

This interaction with Tia struck me for two reasons.

First, this is what I'd consider "a penny's worth of knowledge." Neither of us knew about this duplicate content information at the outset of our blogging journeys, but we picked it up along the way. Like a penny.

If I add this to some of the other things I've learned about working on the web, it starts to add up. Like pennies turn into dimes, quarters and dollars, this one fact adds to the breadth of knowledge I'm creating as I go along picking up "pennies of knowledge" about being a web genius!

There are always more pennies to pick up, just like there will ALWAYS be more to learn. It's never ending, but the value is greater and greater with each additional "penny."

The second thing that struck me about Tia's messages was the WAY in which she told me this information. She was so kind, and so understanding. She even told me she'd made the same mistake a few weeks earlier!

Doing this made me so much more receptive to hearing about my mistake. It was as if she gave me a "penny's worth of understanding."

"Hey look, I made this mistake, too…just wanted you to know the impact of your action."

What a gift!! How amazing to not only have someone who is honest enough to show me where I might improve, but who also has the humility to share her own mistake as well. Lucky me!

Lesson

Mistakes are… wait for it… a blessing! Weird, I know. But let yourself believe that for just a minute.

Mistakes are like strangers who dropped pennies just before you showed up to find them. Just like picking up a penny can be exciting, fun and add VALUE to your life, so too can learning the lessons brought to you by your mistakes.

Without duplicating the content I'd shared with Tia on another site, I would never have learned that is an online no-no! I might have gone on doing that and damaged site after site because I didn't know any better.

Obviously, I don't set out to make mistakes, but I also no longer fear them or view them as bad things. I try to see the upside. The things I'm learning BECAUSE I made those mistakes!

What are your 2 cents?

- What mistakes have you made that led to valuable learning?
- Where could you take more risks if you stopped being afraid of mistakes?
- Who can you kindly tell about a mistake they've made to help them learn a valuable lesson they'll appreciate and use in the future?

Focus

What You Think About Comes About… So Think About The Good Stuff!

S ince the early days of The Penny Project, almost every time I leave the house I find at least one penny…usually more than that! In fact, I've become so vigilant about penny finding, I am hard pressed NOT to find a penny whenever I walk out of my front door. My eyes are always scanning!

My friends have grown accustomed to talking with me while I am looking elsewhere "elsewhere" usually being somewhere between the sidewalk and the street. Talk about one's mind being in the gutter! People are constantly amazed at how many pennies I find.

One of the people most amazed by my penny finding successes is my life coach, Tim. Despite working together on and off for 14 years, we rarely get to see one other since we live in different states. As luck would have it, one day he happened to be in the DC area for business and asked if I was free for dinner. I jumped at the chance to see him in person and drove out to meet him that evening. It turns out our decision to meet for dinner was the LAST easy thing we'd do that night.

When I got to Tim's hotel, he told me there had been a water main break that had forced the hotel's restaurant to close down the kitchen. Even though our stomachs were already growling, we didn't think this was a big problem. I was more concerned about introducing Tim to my dented, hubcap-less, 1997 Geo Prizm, to be honest! But, I figured he'd get over it once we got somewhere with good food!

We asked the hotel for a local restaurant recommendation and off we went. We drove several miles only to find out that the restaurant was closed. Since it was located in a strip mall, we decided to walk over to another restaurant. It was also closed, but it had a sign explaining that all the restaurants in the entire county were shut down because of the water main break.

We quickly realized we needed a plan B if we wanted to eat dinner together that night.

Not one to be deterred by such small details as the unavailability of a formal restaurant, I suggested we hit the grocery store, buy food that wouldn't require cooking, and then go back to the hotel bar where we could have a drink with our food.

Tim looked a bit uncertain but trusted that I knew what I was doing.

We walked over to the supermarket and I grabbed one of the little hand baskets. Upon entering the store, I was immediately distracted by a penny on the floor. Naturally, I rushed over to pick it up while Tim wandered off in the aisles. At the exact moment he realized I wasn't walking next to him, I popped up from behind the display where I'd found the penny and proudly showed off my find while asking him, "What are you in the mood for?"

"I don't know. My wife usually does all the shopping," answered Tim, still slightly thrown off by my side- adventure.

It wasn't until this point I realized he was a fish out of water. One look at his face and I could see he certainly didn't do the family's grocery shopping. I began wondering if he'd even been IN a supermarket since he got married!

Laughing at the irony that I was now guiding my coach, we headed to the produce section and I suggested an assortment of veggies we could dip in hummus (because let's face it, EVERYTHING is better with hummus!). Tim agreed with my idea, and we got some carrots, celery, and cherry tomatoes.

"What else?" I asked.

No answer.

"How about some cheese and crackers?" I asked. "I'm sure the hotel kitchen will loan us a knife. Lord knows they won't be using them tonight!"

So we grabbed the cheese, crackers and a few more items, and then headed to the checkout lanes.

It's worth noting here that checkout lanes are typically a goldmine! Think about it people are digging through their wallets (hence an opportunity for change to drop) and wanting to get to the car before the ice cream melts (causing a lack of concern for pennies left behind). I LOVE checkout lanes!

As predicted, when we approached the checkout lanes, I saw a wayward penny and rushed to pick it up. I then began to scan each lane as we walked by, looking to see if there were other pennies I could swoop in and grab along the way. I ended up with 4 cents by the time we left the supermarket. True, 4 cents may not sound like a lot to you, but it starts to add up, trust me! Tim said he'd never seen anything like that before and thought I must be pretty powerful to manifest pennies with such regularity. I thought, "If I'm that powerful, I need to up my game and manifest $20 bills, or at least something bigger than a penny!"

Once we got back to the hotel and sidled up to the restaurant bar with our groceries, Tim and I ordered some beers and settled into a fantastic conversation. For me, it was like a 3-hour coaching call all for the low price of the gas to get there. I was in heaven!

We talked about all sorts of things life, business, family, dreams, you name it. It was a wonderful evening and I was happy that I braved the DC traffic to make the trip.

Little did I know that Tim was also affected by the events of that evening. The whole grocery store experience was way out of his norm. He later told me that he ended up sharing the story with several friends and clients. He also used the penny finding as a point of reference during some of our later coaching calls.

Here is the part of the story where I confess that one of the topics I often wanted coaching on was why I couldn't find a boyfriend.

DC is not the easiest city in the world in which to date, and I was just not having any luck with the long-suffering, long-distance relationship I was trying desperately to hold onto.

Finally, one day Tim asked me, "Are you as focused on finding a good man as you are on finding pennies?"

Now THAT gave me pause.

Finally, I said, "No. I guess I'm not."

And then I began the tired string of explanations and excuses.

"But DC is different from other cities, Tim. Everyone here is about 'who you know' and what you can do for them."

"Excuses," he replied. "How often do you think about pennies?"

"At least a few times a day." Pause. "OK, probably more like a few times an hour," I admitted.

"Right, you have your spreadsheet, you're always finding them, you BELIEVE you're going to find them, and BOOM there they are! Are you doing anything even remotely close to that with men?"

I got his point. Up until that moment, I never left the house believing that there were good men out there the way I KNEW that there would be pennies. Not to mention the fact that when I did think about dating, which wasn't very often, it wasn't really where my focus was. In fact, it had NEVER been where my focus was. Suddenly, my lack of a boyfriend, in contrast with my bounty of pennies, made sense.

Armed with this new insight and advice from Tim, I began to shift my focus on finding the GOOD men in DC. As a result, my friends, acquaintances, and even one of my workshop students, began setting me up with single men that they knew and liked. Not to mention another friend who told me about a free online dating web site that also led to some great dates! I ended up meeting five really nice guys in the span of a few months as a result of my new attitude.

Needless to say, my next conversation with Tim was filled with some funny, happy, and positive stories of the new men in my life.

Lesson

You get what you focus on. It doesn't matter if it's something you want or don't want, care about or don't care about, need or don't need. When you spend your time thinking about it, there it is.

Every day I think about pennies. Every trip to the store includes a walk by the checkout lanes it has become part of my routine. Do I always find pennies there? No.

But when I do find them, I know it's because I've focused on doing so. When people are with me at the supermarket, or walking with me down the street, they're amazed at what I find. I'm not amazed. Happy, but not amazed. That's because I know that what they're seeing is the payoff for my consistent focus and belief that I will find pennies at some point.

Simply put, I find pennies because I spend a lot of time focusing on finding pennies. When it came to dating, I found a bunch of not-so-desirable guys because I constantly stated how bad the dating scene was in DC. It took my coach to point out the disparity between my focus on finding pennies versus my focus on finding men for me to see that I needed a new approach.

And once I applied that new approach, new men came into my life. Quality men. Men I am proud to have met and dated.

It's amazing how much better life can be when you decide to place your focus on the good things life has to offer!

What are your 2 cents?

- Where is your focus today?
- Is your focus bringing you the things you want out of life?
- How can you shift your focus to get what you DO want instead of what you DON'T want?

Inconvenient Joy

Why You Should ALWAYS Choose To Turn That Frown Upside Down If The Opportunity Presents Itself

Seems not a day can go by that I don't learn a thing or two from pennies. It's not necessarily just finding a penny that teaches me things; it's contrasting the way I react now with the way I would have in the past.

Let me explain.

One day I decided to swing by the grocery store after my morning meeting at Starbucks. The store is only about 6 blocks from my house. I'd even remembered to bring my cloth shopping bags so I wouldn't have to use plastic ones. It felt like the perfect opportunity to grab a few items on my shopping list.

But two items turned into five. And when I walked by the meat counter and saw chicken for $1.99/pound, I knew I had to stock up. Ten pounds later, I headed for the dairy section where I had to get regular milk (for my parents' upcoming visit) and soy milk (for a good friend stopping by that afternoon).

I made it to the checkout lanes — but just barely! That basket had gotten heavy in a hurry. Not to mention the weather had turned unseasonably warm. Too warm for the coat I was wearing, which I stashed in one of the grocery bags to avoid a heat stroke on my return trip.

All of this added up to me looking like a haggard shopper who might not make it out of the store, let alone all the way home!

As I walked away from the self checkout aisle, I immediately spotted a penny in one of the other lanes. I didn't even think about whether or not I should unburden myself to pick up the penny. I simply set down my bags, picked up the penny, and stashed it in my back pocket. Then I re-burdened myself with the massive amounts of chicken and milk I'd just purchased before continuing my journey home.

After leaving the store, I found six more pennies. Each penny was found separately, which meant repeating the process of setting down my stuff to free up my hands for coin collecting.

At no time did I think to myself, "Is it really worth setting down all this stuff and picking it back up just so I can pick up ONE little penny?" This project had taught me the value of a penny, and it had nothing to do with buying power.

With each penny I find, I am reminded of the abundance I have in my life. I've got a roof over my head, a family that loves me (even if they are a bit confused by my quirks), great friends, work that I love, and enough money in the bank to cover an emergency or two. And on top of that, I have a whole army of penny finders out there who continually inspire me with their stories, notes, well wishes, and handfuls of money!

But it wasn't always this way. Ask anyone who knew me before I found "Zen & The Art of Pennies."

In my younger days, I had the unique ability to ignore really great opportunities or events to stay ensconced in whatever nasty mood I had fallen into because of some perceived slight or misfortune.

Like the time my boyfriend said he didn't think I deserved a celebration for being signed off as a pilot in command. And to be clear, this "celebration" involved rolling around in mud and having ice water dumped on your head — more of a rite of passage than a party.

I was really hurt. And when I got back from my check ride (the flight test I had to pass in order to be signed off), I was hoping that Mr. Grumpy Pants wasn't going to be there to ruin my fun.

But there he was. And instead of ignoring his nasty, bitter mood, I decided to take it on as my own. So when the celebration DID start — and I saw him standing there being unsupportive — I just went through the motions and focused on the fact that the one person I wanted to be happy for me wasn't.

That's right. Instead of looking around at the dozens of people there to cheer me on and help me celebrate my rite of passage into the role of pilot-in-command, I held tight to my anger and permanently marred the memory of that hard earned accomplishment. Way to stick to my guns, eh? Did I really come out the victor there?

Or, there was the time I got dumped right before my dad's 60th birthday. My mom had rented a houseboat on Lake Mead for the week, big enough for eight people (which meant my sister and I could both bring our boyfriends). Well…half of that last part worked out.

So there I was on a 2-story boat — complete with a hot tub and waterslide on the roof — surrounded by the people I love most in the world. But all I wanted to do was pout about the fact I had been dumped and would probably be single — with cats — for the rest of my life. I was COMPLETELY inconsolable.

Oh, and I secretly (or maybe NOT so secretly) wanted everyone else to be miserable too. Despite my best efforts, they STILL had a great time. This only annoyed me further.

And then, one day, along came The Penny Project. At first, not much in my life changed just because I found a few pennies. For example, when the new shopping complex opened up the street from me, I would often make return trips from the store over-burdened with more merchandise than one should really carry at one time. On those trips, I would actually be upset when I found a penny.

Didn't the Universe know that NOW was not the time to send me a penny? I had stuff in my hands! How dare someone drop a penny right there, right now! Didn't he or she KNOW I was going to be coming by at this moment with arms full of stuff and too busy to pick it up? How rude!

Wait…did I just think that? Was I honestly getting frustrated because something that usually brought me joy didn't come to me in the exact way, with the exact timing, I wanted?

Apparently, I wanted lots of joy in my life — as long as it wasn't inconvenient joy.

But now, no matter where I am or what I'm doing, I can make time to pick up a penny. And once I made that shift, I realized it wasn't such a stretch to leave a bad mood behind and accept the inconvenient joys that sometimes pop up in life. It also turns out that when you stop trying to judge the space and timing of how you receive joy, it really isn't so inconvenient after all!

Lesson

It's easy to be happy when the timing is perfect and you're ready to receive what you want. But how many times in life does that actually happen? In case you've lost count, the answer is "almost never."

The trick is to stop clutching the nasty moods so tightly and to start looking for the things in life that make you want to put them down in favor of being happy.

What a coincidence that the way I learned this lesson was the physical act of putting down heavy bags in order to pick up a penny. Don't we all carry around emotional baggage that we hold onto so tightly that we can't set it down to pick up life's joys?

What are your 2 cents?

- Where are you pinching off opportunities for happiness because you've grown comfortable carrying bags full of misery, anger or discontent?
- How can you begin to set down those bags and pick up something you REALLY want to hold onto?
- How will YOU react the next time the Universe gives you what you want, just not in the way you were hoping to get it?

Chapter 7 / My 2¢ On…

What Others Think of You
Why It's Never As Bad As You Think
It's Going To Be… And Who Cares If It Is?

Hands down, one of the best pieces of advice I've ever gotten came from my life coach, Tim. During a period of extreme frustration in my life when other people's evaluations of my performance mattered a great deal to me, I called him week after week beaten down by the belief that other people didn't think as highly of me as I wanted them to.

What Tim told me back then bounced off me like the old schoolyard saying "I'm rubber, you're glue…"

But 14 years later, after numerous (and ridiculous) penny incidents and a great dinner conversation with two dear friends about the lessons they'd learned from picking up pennies, I can see that what Tim said is absolutely right.

What he told me was so simple, and yet too impossible to believe when I first heard it in the midst of the critiques and feedback I was getting during my first assignment as a new lieutenant in the Army.

"What other people think of you is none of your business."

Like I said, I didn't buy it at the time. And although he'd helped me in many other aspects of my life, I was pretty sure he was off his rocker on this one. The people he was talking about wrote my evaluations. They literally held my career in their hands. How could I NOT be concerned with what they thought of me?

Fast forward ten years.

Even in the realm of my penny-picking-up world, I found I still had concerns about what others thought of me. When they saw me walking down the street with my head down, did they think I lacked confidence?

What DID people think when they saw me scraping up coins out of the gutter? That I actually needed them? That I was odd (and probably had dirty hands)?

Part of me wanted to crow out to every passerby that saw me pick up a penny, "I graduated from West Point and have plenty of money in the bank!!!" Although, that particular approach had me slightly nervous that people would think West Point was turning out a bunch of crazies!

Then one day, an interaction at a local sandwich shop made me rethink all of those thoughts I'd had about what people on the street thought of my penny habits.

I was eating lunch with my girlfriends and noticed two pennies under the table across from us. The table was occupied by some younger, hipper kids also enjoying their lunch. I thought for sure they'd be done before we would and I could dart under the table to pick up the pennies before leaving the restaurant.

No such luck.

After we finished eating, I asked the girls if we could hang out for a few more minutes to see if we could outwait those kids so I could grab the pennies. Clearly, my friends had already accepted my penny obsession, so I had no qualms about telling them I was stalking the pennies under the neighboring table. We waited several minutes until it became clear those kids were hunkered down for awhile and had no plans of vacating their seats.

I had a choice. Did I walk away and leave the two pennies behind for fear of looking stupid in front of these strangers, or did I ask them if I could pop under the table for a moment to snatch up the coins? (NOTE: By this stage in the game, I'd been on bus floors, fished stuff out of gutters, and a whole host of other bizarre places, so crawling under a table seemed relatively minor to me. It was their REACTION I was worried about).

That day, instead of letting my "what will they think?" mentality get the better of me, I opted to go for the pennies.

Certain that I was going to get a whole lot of attitude and mockery from these kids, I approached the table and said, "I'm sorry, but there's some pennies under your table and I'm kind of obsessed with picking up all the money I find for charity. Do you mind if I crawl under there and grab them?"

One of the kids looked at me in all seriousness and said, "Man, there's a recession going on! You gotta do what you gotta do. Take 'em!"

Not only was it not the response I was expecting, it was actually funny and somewhat encouraging! Why hadn't I just done this in the first place instead of making my friends waste 10 minutes sitting around? Was I really THAT afraid of what those kids would think of me?

Turns out that yes, I had been worried about the impression I'd leave. What a waste of energy!

After that invaluable learning experience, I went on to notice that when I did ask someone, "Pardon me, you're standing on a penny… do you mind if I grab it?" or "These pennies on the bus dash board, do they belong to anyone? Can I snatch them up for charity?" not only did I NOT get a negative, surly response, but I usually got a smile!

Some people even went as far as to "accidentally" drop a few extra pennies that I could pick up for the cause!

Looking back, I realized I could not think of a single incident in which the person I asked was anything but nice and supportive about my penny quest. In fact, many of them ended up asking how they could keep track of my stories and fundraising progress!

These days, I don't feel the need to explain myself at all when I swoop under someone's foot in the checkout lanes at Target or grab a penny from under an empty bus seat (unless I feel like I'm invading an individual's personal space — explaining myself seems warranted in those situations!). I've come to realize that what my coach said all those years ago was right.

What people think of me really ISN'T any of my business!

The fact is, I know why I'm picking up pennies. I know I'm not poor, crazy, dirty, or lacking confidence. Does it really matter if a random person in the Target checkout line knows it, too?

And what's more, the sillier and crazier I get with ways to find and pick up pennies, the more fun I have. Not to mention how much fun the people around me have, too!

Certainly there are those who are not amused, don't approve, and think I should be committed to some kind of institution. But these days, the only opinions about me that I care about are my own. And all of those seem to be just fine!

Lesson

Don't waste your time worrying about what other people are thinking.

a) You'll almost never get it right
b) It's rarely (if ever) as bad as you think it's going to be
c) Most likely they're so concerned with what others are thinking of THEM, they don't notice you
d) What they think doesn't matter any way

Don't spend another second of your life worrying about what other people are thinking of you. Spend your energy on making sure that what you think of yourself feels good and reflects who you are. Figure that out and the rest of the world will follow!

What are your 2 cents?

- What are the biggest fears you have about what others will think of you?
- How do those reflect the ways in which YOU judge others?
- Where can you shift your thinking to feel good about yourself instead of worrying about what others think of you?

The Ripple Effect
Why It Really Is Better To Say Something Nice
Or Say Nothing At All

It's funny how when you decide to do something and fully commit yourself to it people and resources seem to pop out of the woodwork to help you. Such has been my experience with turning my penny stories into a book.

On the first day that I sat down to begin working on my 34-day book writing challenge, I had plans to meet up with an old army buddy, Mike. Mike was the non-commissioned officer (NCO) in charge of Operations at the very first unit I went to after completing flight school. He was a true professional and someone I really enjoyed working with.

But as is apt to happen in the army, you move from unit to unit, get caught up in what you're currently doing, and lose touch with some of the folks who made a big impression on you early on. At least, that was the case until the advent of Facebook!

Thanks to Facebook and Mike's job bringing him to DC for a conference, we were able to meet for coffee and catch up on the past eight years of our lives.

We met at a Starbucks on one of the coldest, windiest days of the year. I mean, it was FREEZING! As soon as I walked in and saw him, we hugged and then made a bee-line for the counter so we could order some warm drinks to defrost our frozen little hands.

Given that a counter is similar to a checkout lane in my penny hunting world, I was on the prowl and immediately spotted a penny on the floor. I picked it up and explained to Mike, "I have this whole thing about picking up pennies for charity."

"Yeah, I know…I've seen it on your Facebook page," he replied with a chuckle.

How perfect! It hadn't occurred to me that he actually might have been paying attention to my constant penny chatter online:

"Penny, penny, DIME!"
or
"It was a 42 cent day…WAHOO!"

It dawned on me that anyone who is my friend on Facebook would know about my little obsession without my having to explain it. Fantastic!

Excited with this new insight, I slipped the penny in my pocket and we found some comfy chairs to sit in while we caught up.

It's funny how eight years feels like the blink of an eye whenever I sit down with someone I knew in the army. There's just something about that bond created by our time in the military that makes everything else fall into place.

We sat and chatted for hours and caught up on all the folks we knew from Fort Campbell, where we'd first met 10 years before. We also talked about the ups and downs of life, the difference between civilian life and the army, and what we're hoping for next in our life journeys. This was certainly not your typical afternoon chat in Starbucks!

When I mentioned I'd just started writing a book about the lessons I've learned from my pennies, Mike told me he'd read the guest blog post I'd written about how pennies taught me to appreciate the little joys in life (the introduction to this book).

It took me a second to figure out how he'd even gotten the link. I thought I'd only sent it to my core list of penny contributors when I did my monthly update. I'd forgotten that I'd posted it on my Facebook page, too.

He went on to tell me that he'd forwarded the link to a friend who was having a rough time of it lately as a means of getting her to see "the bigger picture" in her life. He told me she'd really enjoyed it and said that reading the penny story helped her see some of the little things in her life that were going well.

Who knew?!

Somewhat worn out by three years of updates, many of my devoted (but insanely busy) penny finders told me they'd gotten the recent update but hadn't had time to read the blog post. I figured if they wouldn't read it, then no one would.

But here was Mike telling me he'd enjoyed the post so much that he actually passed it on to someone else he thought could benefit from reading it as well. I never would have known this were it not for Facebook, his conference, and a few free hours spent drinking gingerbread lattes at Starbucks!

This revelation got me thinking. Who else might have read my blog post that I didn't know about? How big was the "ripple effect" I'd created with my story? I'd been telling it for years, but it never occurred to me to share my story as a guest blogger until Tia asked if I'd be willing to write it up for her blog.

Her audience had given me lots of great feedback. Another friend asked if she could post the story on her website, too. Now I found that someone unknown to me and unrelated to either of those blogs got comfort from my story via a link passed on by a mutual friend of ours. What an amazing tool technology is!

Lesson

What you do in life, whether you know it or not, has a ripple effect. Whether you throw a proverbial penny kind words, happy thoughts, positive feedback in the pool , or throw something less nice hate-filled words, anger, negativity the ripples you create WILL reach others. The good news is YOU have the power. YOU get to choose what kind of ripples you want to make.

So how will you create your ripples? Will you find the 'pennies' in your life and share them with others? Or will you ignore them and focus on something less positive because that's what everyone else is doing (like talking about the bad economy because it's on EVERY news channel)?

Be careful what you choose — when enough ripples get together, they create a wave. And waves have the power to create big change. So be sure to use your ripple for good, not evil!

What are your 2 cents?

- What are you throwing into the pool of life to create YOUR ripples?
- What legacy will your ripple effect leave behind?
- What kind of waves do you want to be a part of?
- What kind of waves do you want to leave behind for the next generation?

On Being Messy
Why The Crazy Things You Do
Are The Ones You'll Actually Remember

A while back, I decided that I loved working with my life coach so much that I wanted to become one. I convinced my company to send me to training classes. During those five months of vigorous training and practicing, I not only learned how to coach others, but also got some amazing coaching from my classmates in return.

One of the most significant things I learned in my training was the importance of knowing your values.

'Values' is such a serious word that I think it often puts people off a bit. Words like truth, character, and fortitude come to mind. It's all a bit daunting!

Fortunately, one of my coaching instructors shared with us one of the core values he lives by. He calls the value 'Chocolate.'

Yes, you read correctly. Chocolate! And it's EXACTLY what it sounds like. The man loves chocolate.

Only he knows for certain the true meaning of chocolate as a guiding principle of how he lives his life. But by sharing his chocolate-covered value with our class, he gave us permission to come up with our own nutty ideals, allowing us to leave behind any thought that we had to be 100% serious about the task at hand.

This was a great relief to me. I'd spent over a decade in and around the army. Although I appreciated and respected the Army Values (Loyalty, Duty, Respect, Selfless Service, Honor, Integrity, and Personal Courage), they left little room for creativity and fun.

Over the course of my training, I tapped into my internal beliefs and discovered that I had a core value called "Cake Hands."

It took me a while to define and name the initially nebulous belief. However, I got great clarity on it when my coach, Tim, told me that he often asked groups he facilitated for permission to be messy. That way, no one had to worry about mistakes or missteps. They could just focus on accomplishing the task at hand even if it got a bit hairy at times or looked like the proverbial "ugly baby."

Tim's statement triggered the memory of something that had happened at cheer camp my sophomore year in high school.

The JV and varsity squads attended camp together at the University of California Santa Barbara. I was a nerdy sophomore albeit a coordinated one who knocked the judges socks off at tryouts who really admired the cool junior and senior girls on the varsity squad. They were pretty and popular, and as the new kid on the cheerleading block, I really looked up to them.

One night, after a long day of dancing to 90's pop music in the sun, we all assembled in the common area of our dorm to celebrate the birthdays of a few girls on the squad. The advisors had gotten a big sheet cake, which sat on the coffee table in the middle of the room.

As I walked down the hall to join the celebration, I noticed one of my favorite varsity girls sitting on the floor directly in front of the cake. As the teams filtered into the room, this girl got a devilish look in her eye. Just as the last few girls walked in, she sat up straight, held her arms out with her fingers bent into claw-like configurations, and screamed, "Cake hands!"

Before I knew it, all hell had broken loose. This girl was tearing into the cake like a Tasmanian devil. Frosting was flying and 20 other girls were following her lead hoping to get a hand on some cake before it was all gone. Each girl had cake on her face, cake in her hair, and crumbs were shooting around the room like a Hollywood food fight scene.

I can't recall if the advisors were amused or not, but I do know we didn't go to bed that night until every last cake crumb was cleaned up.

I also know that I don't recall many birthday parties from high school (or any other time for that matter). But I can recall with great clarity that particular celebration.

My "cake hands" memory came to mind again recently when my best friend from high school came to see me while I was in town visiting my parents.

We'd been enjoying a few days of Christmas shopping, visiting friends, playing Scrabble, and other assorted Karina and Leslie type activities. It was a lovely visit, but nothing out of the ordinary.

One night after stopping by to see a friend's new baby girl, we were heading home to have dinner with my folks. My mom asked us to stop by the store and grab something on our way home, which we gladly did.

On the way out of the parking lot, I was looking out the window as Karina rolled up to the intersection. "Hey, there's a penny!" I said.

Karina didn't reply.

"Wait…there's another one. And another one, and…oh my gosh, there's a dime! I have to jump out and get these!"

"Wait!" she shouted frantically. "The light's about to turn green you can't get out!"

Sure enough, the light turned and we had to move in order to avoid an angry cacophony of honking horns behind us.

As we pulled out of the intersection I looked over at her and said, "Karina, we have to go back!"

She laughed.

I laughed, too. "I think it's really cute that you think I'm kidding."

"Are you serious? You really want to go back and jump out of the car in an intersection to pick up a few pennies?"

"It was more than a few pennies! I saw at least two dimes."

"Do you really think that's a great idea? At night? In your dark jeans and black trench coat?" she asked, hoping (I think) to talk a little sense into me.

But there's no talking sense into me when cents are involved. "I'll be fine. Make a U-turn when you can."

Still not all together sure I wasn't going to become a tragic pedestrian death statistic, she turned around and asked what the plan was.

"Ok, here's what I want you to do. Take a right at the intersection and stop long enough for me to hop out of the car. You continue on to the parking lot where you'll turn around and come back to get in the left turn lane at the light. While you are turning around, I will cross the median, grab the money, and be ready by the time you get there."

Being one of my best penny finders, having seen me do ridiculous things in the name of pennies before, and knowing there was no point in arguing, she dropped me off and went on to turn the car around as I had asked.

I immediately sprung into action making sure to get eye contact with the drivers so they wouldn't miss me as I bent down to pick up all the change I'd seen. Would they think I was stupid and probably a little crazy? Absolutely! Did I think they were going to run me down because they didn't see me? No way.

Just as I swooped up the last dime, Karina pulled up next to me and I hopped in.

"Are you happy now?" she sarcastically joked.

"Um, yeah," I said as I showed her my two handfuls of change.

"Holy crap!! You weren't kidding. That's a ton of pennies!" she said as she burst out laughing and high-fived me for my efforts.

"And two dimes and two nickels! I told you it was a lot of change," I said as I returned her high-five and laughed at the new lengths I'd gone to in the name of penny-finding.

I immediately called home to report the big find, Mom and Dad are equally avid penny finders, and explained why we were running a little behind.

When I got home and showed off the big score, we counted it up and found it totaled 53 cents, which is a big day in my penny-finding world. Oddly, my parents were proud of me. And, although "proud" is not the word I'm sure Karina would use to describe how she felt about the incident, she was still laughing and is probably not going to soon forget the night she played driver for the great penny pick-up.

Which story do you think makes for a better memory:

1. I was driving home with my crazy friend who is obsessed, by the way, with finding pennies on the ground AND has dragged the rest of us into her nutty obsession when she saw a pile of pennies in the intersection. We had to pull away because the light turned green. But then she insisted I go back. I thought she was kidding at first, but then I realized that she was TOTALLY serious. So I drove her back to the intersection where the pennies were, and she jumped out of the car and dashed across the median to pick up whatever it was she had seen. I kept thinking, "Who cares that much about a few pennies?!" While she picked them up, I turned the car around in the parking lot and came back to get her. As I pulled up, she hopped back in the car and held out a huge handful of pennies! 53 cents!! I burst out laughing because who throws that much money out in an intersection? And who comes along and picks it up?! The whole thing was hilarious!

or...

2. I drove my friend home and nothing happened.

Lesson

Don't be so concerned with perfection. Or cleanliness. Or doing it right the first time. Or avoiding mistakes. That's boring. Give yourself the permission to be messy. Screw some stuff up and make memories, for God's sake!

What are your funniest memories? Are they about the same weekly Tuesday night dinner where your mom made meatloaf? Or are they about the Thanksgiving dinner where your aunt had too much to drink and couldn't stop chuckling to herself as she spelled a string of dirty words in Boggle?

Life is meant to be enjoyed. So once in a while, hatch a crazy scheme, get that gleam in your eye, and make a "cake hands" kind of memory!

What are your 2 cents?

- Think of a favorite memory. Does it come from an experience inside or outside "the norm?"
- What mistakes or missteps in your life have turned out to be opportunities?
- Which memories might actually be indications of your own hidden values?

Dedication
Why It's Better To Do A Little Bit A Lot, Than A Lot A Little Bit

About three weeks before finding the $20 bill that got me thinking about picking up pennies, I took a class on facilitation skills called The Effective Facilitator.

The class knocked my socks off. Not only was the instructor amazing, but the material was incredible AND we got six chances to practice what we were learning during the course of the 4-day class. I walked away thinking, "THESE are my people. I want to be a facilitator!"

I went back to work and asked my boss if I could facilitate our department's upcoming off-site strategy session. It was an all-day affair and I knew it would give me the chance to use a bunch of the techniques and tools I'd learned in the class. Plus, I wanted to show her that her training dollars were being put to good use. A little self-promotion never hurt anyone!

She agreed to my proposal and I spent the next week prepping for the meeting to make sure we'd walk away with the deliverables she needed.

To explain what happened during our off-site, it would help to know a few things about me. First, I've always been an "all or nothing" kind of girl. Some people like to say my switch only has two speeds: A) "100 miles an hour with my hair on fire" and B) STOP!

This has been true all my life whether it was about school, work, or how I dressed myself.

When I first got out of the army, I would show up at my sister's house and she would ask, "What on EARTH are you wearing?"

"What?!" I'd reply incredulously, not sure why she had a beef with my outfit.

"Leslie…I know you've spent the last 7 years in uniform, but that doesn't mean you need to take each opportunity you get dressed to make up for all those times you couldn't wear accessories. You look like a Claire's Boutique threw up on you."

She was right. I had bracelets on both arms, big dangly earrings, multiple necklaces, two or three rings on each hand, hair accessories, a huge handbag (with matching shoes and belt, of course), and probably a broach or two to top it all off. I was just so excited to wear all of these fun things — which I wasn't allowed to put on while the army had me dressing like a tree — that I went crazy and wore them all at once.

That first off-site meeting was the same way.

I introduced every facilitation technique I had in my bag of tricks. I arranged the room in just the right way. I created a set of ground rules for the group to follow. I had colored markers and sticky pads for brainstorming exercises. You name it, I did it.

Overall, the meeting was a big success and my boss agreed to let me do more facilitation as part of my job description. Judging by some of the looks I'd gotten during our myriad of exercises, the group was a little overwhelmed by all the bells and whistles, but they knew my heart was in the right place.

I realized I probably needed to tone it down a bit and choose one or two techniques to employ in future meetings until I figured out what worked best for me.

The course I had taken broke facilitation into ten basic principles. I figured if I could focus on one of those each month for the sessions I'd be facilitating, I would get better over time.

So that's what I did. I looked for every opportunity I could to facilitate (work meetings, community groups, my condo board discussions, etc.) and continued building my skills with each session.

During this time, I was also enjoying the fun I'd created with my penny spreadsheet. Each day, I'd walk to work with my eyes peeled for pennies on the sidewalk. I became pretty good at spotting them and, as time wore on, other people started to wonder what I was doing.

A few months in, my friend Illeny became my first supporter. I had never planned on this being a project for anyone other than me, so I had to figure out what to do with the pennies she gave me. I decided to add the change she gave me to the daily total and create a separate column for her called "Illeny's Pennies" (it rhymed AND kept our totals separate so I'd still know how much I found).

As The Penny Project grew (part of which I owe to my friend Michele for helping me title it "The Penny Project"), so did my facilitation skills. Ten months after completing the first course, my boss sent me to the advanced facilitation training offered by the same company.

Little did I know, THIS would be where my facilitation journey would really begin. The CEO of the company, Michael Wilkinson, was the instructor of that particular course. It turned out that he thought I was a pretty good facilitator and he asked me to consider joining the company's core team of contractors.

I was excited but extremely nervous. Michael was a master! And I'd taken the class from their core team contractor in DC. He was also amazing. I was happy to think that Michael thought I had some raw skill, but I knew I was nowhere near the realm of the other facilitators they already employed. I also knew that if I didn't accept his offer, I'd NEVER be as good as they were.

I agreed to test for a spot on the core team and, if I passed, to get certified to teach the very course that had gotten me so excited about facilitation in the first place.

Months of studying ensued. All the while, I continued picking up my pennies and enlisting new penny-finders along the way. At the end of the first year, we'd collected over $85. Not too shabby!

As I rolled into year two of both my facilitation and penny finding, I did indeed pass the test to become a core team member and became certified to teach The Effective Facilitator. That same year I also took on some tough facilitation jobs inside my company as we faced an uncertain economy and had to make difficult decisions about which programs to keep and which ones would have to be cut.

Through it all, I kept up with the penny finding AND with studying the basics of facilitation. I attended conferences, read books, and tried to make myself an expert on facilitation techniques and group dynamics. On the penny front, I mentioned my project at one of the conferences I attended and before I knew it, someone handed me a bag full of $75 worth of pocket change from the rest of the attendees. Now THAT was exciting!

Year two hit a bit of turbulence when the very cuts I was helping to facilitate at my company ended up affecting me personally. I was laid off from my job. I finished the year with lots of pennies (over $305), but no certainty about what my professional future would hold.

After a lot of thought, I opted to go out on my own and become a full-time contract trainer and facilitator. There were a few scary moments, and it was certainly a life changing experience being on my own rather than working under the safety of a large company. But, after the first few months of adjusting to my new professional lifestyle, I began to find my footing.

At just about the same time I started to feel as if I'd come into my own as a facilitator, I noticed that The Penny Project bank account had reached $500. It was quite a milestone considering that the bulk of the money came to me in one and two-cent increments!

In fact, it was in noticing that the account had reached $500 that I took stock of where I was as a facilitator. I no longer needed to imitate the masters I had learned from. I had discovered my own style and was in the process of becoming my own version of a master.

I'd started facilitating and collecting pennies at the same time. And although I didn't realize it then, each facilitation skill I practiced was like a penny I added to the spreadsheet. I was a little wiser and a little more experienced with each session I led. One might also say a little richer.

And so, as I hit $500 and decided to find something worthwhile to do with all these formerly wayward pennies, I also hit my stride as a trainer and facilitator. Ironically, I now tell this story each time I instruct The Effective Facilitator class.

I tell my students to facilitate EVERY chance they get. I tell them to never pass up an opportunity to use the principles they learned during the course, and never to think that anything they do as facilitators doesn't add value to their overall abilities. Yes, even the mistakes are pennies. In fact, they're more like quarters, teaching us quickly things we don't want to repeat.

Lesson

A yoga instructor once told me, "It's better to do a little bit a lot than it is to do a lot a little bit." I was a bit confused until he broke it down for me like this:

Imagine for a second you were trying to get fit and wanted to do so by running. You would be much better served to run a few miles every day than you would be to sit around all month and then hop up and run an ultra-marathon. While two miles may not seem like much, if you did it every day for a month, you'd have run 60 miles.

Anything in life you want to be good at works the same way. Make a daily habit of filling your life's bank with the pennies of your life's purpose. This may be your vocation (like facilitation was for me), or it could be something you're passionate about and want to work towards mastering (who knew my passion would be pennies?!).

Whatever it is, do the things that will help you understand your field in new and different ways every day. Read books about it. Go to conferences. Seek out opportunities to partner with people whom you respect and want to learn from. Before you know it, you'll have built expertise one experience (or penny) at a time.

Think of it this way:

If you repeated this day 365 times would you be closer to your goals in a year?

If the answer is yes, then you're on the right track! If the answer is no, consider the one or two things you can start doing TODAY to make sure you're closer to your dreams in a year.

What are your 2 cents?

- What daily habits would move you closer to where you want to be in 365 days?
- What daily habits are actually moving you FURTHER from where you want to be?
- What are the things you can start doing "a little bit of a lot" rather than "a lot of a little bit?"

Just Being You
Why You Know You've Got A Good Thing Going
When Your Story Becomes Stranger Than Fiction

I've already told you that I share The Penny Project story and its parallels to my facilitation career with the students I teach in The Effective Facilitator class.

What I didn't tell you is that they don't always believe me.

The first time I told the story, I was teaching a public class in Dallas, TX. I told the students about The Penny Project on day 3 as we wrapped up the material and prepared for their final presentations on day 4.

After I let the class go, people scattered to the four winds to organize their materials. Nothing strikes fear in adult learners like getting up in front of a roomful of their peers and practicing skills they're still trying to learn. Hence their departures like roaches when the lights come on. They wanted to leave quickly to maximize their stress time about what to do for their 15-minute taped sessions.

I ended up going to dinner that night with one of the students to talk about facilitation opportunities. When we got to the restaurant, I found a couple of pennies that, of course, I picked up. This amused my companion to no end, especially when he found a few pennies himself on our way back to the car!

The next morning I came in early, as I do each day of the class, to get the room set up and be ready to kick off on time. When my new fellow penny finder arrived, we had enough time before class that I thought it would be fun to pull up the penny tracking spreadsheet and show him where he fell in the order of things.

I put the spreadsheet up on the big screen at the front of the room and showed him where his four pennies fit in. As people filtered into the room, I continued explaining some of the nuances of the spreadsheet.

First, there's your basic date and amount sections, which are divided into months. The sheet automatically sums the total for each month, so I don't have to worry about the complexity of higher math. There's a separate section that shows how much each penny finder has turned in, broken down by the number of coins other than pennies included in his or her total. There's even a section for foreign money that is tracked separately since we don't allow people to declare their own exchange rates.

Then there are the fancy elements like a color-coded graph showing the sub-categories in the total amount collected:

- Found Money
- Donations
- Fundraising (like the mini-fund drive my table-mates did that got me $75 at a conference)
- Interest
- Accounts Receivable (this is the money I've been told about via text or e-mail but have not yet received)

The more I talked about the spreadsheet, the more people wanted to be part of it. One student who'd come from Japan to take the class gave me a few Yen. A few others gave me pennies they'd found that week.

Then another student walked in and asked what we were doing. When I told her I was showing the class the spreadsheet I'd been talking about yesterday she said, "You mean that's for real? I thought you made that up for our benefit to encourage us to keep practicing facilitation techniques like little pennies."

Incredulously I said, "Yes, it's real! Why would I make this up? It makes me sound like a total geek!"

"It just seemed too perfect to hit $500 right as you were feeling like you knew what you were doing as a facilitator. It sounded fake!"

And that's the moment I knew I was onto a good thing! I'd always loved The Penny Project, but when that woman said it sounded too good to be true, I believed she was right!

That night after class, I thought back on all I'd learned from the pennies. It wasn't that'd I'd saved over $500 one penny at a time. That was definitely cool, but it wasn't my top lesson. Heck, it wasn't even in my top five! I felt like I had my own version of that 80's book "All I Really Need to Know I Learned in Kindergarten." Only, all I had learned was from pennies!

And as I thought back over the lessons, I realized I'd shared them with a lot of people along the way. What really struck me was that I'd gotten $75 at a conference by just telling the story, and the reason I was able to collect over $500 was because I couldn't stop talking about the dang pennies. And whenever I talked about them, people wanted to hear more!

And now, here I was telling the story to my students because it really was a perfect way to help them see that all the little things we practice as facilitators do add up to making us masterful meeting leaders. My personal project had crossed over to have professional relevance. That had never happened to me before!

Since then, the story has remained part of my repertoire when I teach that class. Or any other class for that matter. The principle remains the same.

And now, in addition to telling my students to continually make small deposits into their vocational piggy banks, I tell them to bring themselves into everything they do, not to keep such separate work and personal lives. The crossover is interesting, and in some cases it's just what is needed to make a point.

Lesson

Take stock of the things in your life that you just can't help getting excited about. Share the stories that you can't wait to share with someone because they make you laugh, and when you're laughing, it makes others laugh right along with you. That kind of energy is contagious and we could all use a little more energy. Yes, even in the workplace.

Make a list, check it twice. What are the things that bring you joy and light you up? Even if they're silly, write them down! Find a way to share them with people and see if your enthusiasm doesn't spread.

Remember, I tell people stories about picking up pennies out of the gutter and think they're quite hilarious. If they haven't dragged me off to the loony bin yet, you'll be just fine!

What are your 2 cents?

- Think of someone you know with contagious energy. What makes that person so engaging?
- What do you love to talk about, even when no one is listening?
- In what ways can you share your passions with others not only to light their sparks, but to keep yours lit as well?!

Balance

Why It Might Be Better To Ditch The Idea of Work-Life Balance and Just Embrace Your Imbalanced Life

Often times, as a facilitator and speaker, people come to me knowing they want me to speak to their groups, but they don't know WHAT they want me to speak about. Usually, they've seen me present at a previous course or conference and they connect with my style or energy, but they are unsure as to which topics in my repertoire would suit their audiences best.

Sometimes, I give them a list of topics I've spoken about before and they choose one that will work for their environment. Other times, we kick around ideas and end up developing new material based on the intersection of where my areas of expertise meet the needs of their groups. THOSE are my favorite kinds of presentations.

The latter is what happened when my friend Frances called to ask me if I would speak to a group she coordinated called the Women's Executive Forum, who were offering a lunch & learn program for female executives in the association and nonprofit communities.

I started by offering Frances some of the things I am frequently asked to talk about. "I could do a presentation on communication styles using either the DiSC or Myers-Briggs tool."

"No. We've heard all of that. I want something different."

"Well…I'm doing some life coach training right now," I continued. "I could do something from the recent class I just took on balance."

"Great. Just what I DON'T need: Another person telling me how to have a more balanced life."

"Well…what holes do you have in the overall program this year that I could help you fill?" I asked, hoping to get more of what she did want than what she didn't want.

"I wish someone would talk about the opposite of a balanced life. Like how to just deal with the imbalance."

"Hmm. What if we went with something like that? This balance class is really about shifting perspectives. What if we made the topic about learning to embrace your imbalanced life?"

"Tell me more," Frances said.

I had to think fast — I was making this up as our conversation flowed. "Well…maybe chaos and imbalance aren't such bad things. What if we did some exercises to get the participants thinking of where imbalance has helped them in certain areas of their lives?"

As we continued to talk, we came up with the framework for what sounded like a pretty interesting class. I told Frances I'd play around with it and get an agenda to her in a few weeks.

Then I did what I always do when I need good ideas and a creative spark. I called my mommy.

One of my facilitation mentors once taught a class my mom attended. When she got in front of the room and did her presentation, he looked at her and said, "Well I guess I know where Leslie gets it from!" Apparently the apple hadn't fallen far from the tree.

Being two peas from the same facilitation pod, I often find inspiration in mulling over new ideas with my mom.

So we threw around some ideas and together we came up with some pretty creative ways of looking at balance vs. imbalance. From that conversation, I was able to put together a fun, interactive program I was sure Frances would love.

With a few minor edits, the program was approved as I'd submitted it. This was very exciting given this was really my first foray into developing my own program from scratch. I'd done some customization to existing material in the past, but this was the first one I'd come up with all on my own. OK…on my own with the help of my mom.

The week before I presented the program, I was watching highlights from that day's stage of the Tour de France. There was a piece about Lance Armstrong and other top athletes. While I watched it, I had a thought.

Does anyone ever tell Lance Armstrong to be more balanced?!

I thought back to a piece I'd seen during the Olympics about Michael Phelps' daily routine while in training. It basically consisted of eating, sleeping, and swimming. Again I wondered, does anyone tell HIM to be more balanced?

These questions got me really excited about the presentation. Apparently, I wasn't alone…

The day of the event, I showed up to find the session had double the amount of participants of the normal lunch programs. Clearly, women wanted to talk about imbalance!

The program went splendidly and most of the feedback indicated people could have talked about this for several more hours! The topic and format of the workshop had definitely struck a nerve.

This experience became the foundation for a program I wanted to start called Lead Like a Girl, which focuses on helping women tap into their authentic leadership styles — including how to avoid the trap of thinking you always have to be balanced!

Months went by and one morning I was awakened by a phone call that my caller ID listed as "Ohio." How can one not answer when an entire state beckons?

On the other end of the line was an old friend I hadn't spoken to in ages. The funny thing was she wasn't really calling just to talk to me. She called to get more information about my Lead Like a Girl project. I found this particularly fascinating because it was still in development and I hadn't started advertising it yet. Funny how quickly word travels when you mention things on your Facebook page!

And so we chatted about the program and how I might come to speak at the women's network in her organization. When I told her the whole thing was based on a workshop I'd created about embracing your imbalanced life, she loved it.

"That might be exactly what we need! Women around here are always trying to figure out how to have a better work-life balance."

I told her my theory about learning to love the imbalance for what it offers and shared with her my thought about Michael Phelps. "Do you think anyone ever tells him to be more balanced? Of course not — he's got 9 gold medals! He's the picture of American success. That kind of success DEMANDS people to be out of balance. Our problem is we want success of that magnitude AND balance all at the same time."

"Leslie, you should write about THAT in your book!" she said before we wrapped up work talk and spent a few minutes catching up on the kids and what we'd been up to.

After we hung up the phone, I realized she might be right. When it comes to embracing imbalance, the pennies have taught me well.

Let's take a look at a few ways my scales tip ever so slightly to the crazy side of imbalance where pennies are concerned:

- When I leave my house, I'm ALWAYS scanning for pennies. I could be walking with the President and I'd still be eyes down to the ground, searching for money.
- When I come home, the first thing I see as I walk in the door is my "wall-o-pennies", including my 100 most chewed up pennies from the first year (businesses frame their first dollar, I framed the nastiest pennies I found that year).
- My bedroom window sill is covered with this year's candidates for the 100 worst pennies, and I've got to say, this year's competition is stiff!
- I get texts, emails, and voice messages every day from people who want to report their findings.
- My friends get me penny related gifts (some of which are on the wall-o-pennies).

- I'm constantly finding pennies in the wash that I forgot to remove from my pockets.
- I write about pennies on my blog.
- I write about pennies as a guest blogger for other people's Web sites.
- I talk about pennies with strangers (usually because they're standing on one and I'm trying to recover it for the cause).

Pennies, pennies, pennies! I've become obsessed.

But here's where it gets funny. The thing in my life people want to know about most is how The Penny Project is doing. What's the total so far this year? Where'd we donate the money? Who's ahead on the spreadsheet?

My imbalance has become one of the most interesting facets of my life and personality. And the more I focus on it, the more interesting it seems to become. Interesting enough to write a book about, apparently! (Mom, I do hope you're not the ONLY one reading this!)

So why would I want to get rid of my imbalance? I've found a way to make it fun, make a difference, and to get others involved. Maybe the secret to embracing imbalance is having a good support network.

I'm reminded of something my Dad always used to tell me as a kid. "Whether you think you can or think you can't, you're right." I think he might have been borrowing that thought from Henry Ford, but it's my Dad's voice I hear when it plays in my head.

The same idea goes for imbalance. Whether you think it's good or think it's bad, you're right. What will you decide?

Lesson

Don't be so quick to reject imbalance as a bad thing. There are times in our lives when being out of balance is called for. Sometimes, we even seek it out.

Did you ever think about skipping that wedding you've always wanted because your finances and schedule would be out of whack for a few months? Not likely. Perhaps by embracing imbalance as part of life instead of pushing against it, we'll figure out a way to use its powers for good instead of evil!

What are your 2 cents?

- Where have you voluntarily thrown yourself out of balance in your life?
  - Financially (purchasing a house, paying for an education)
  - Physically (training for a marathon, having a baby)
  - Socially (hosting the family for Thanksgiving, throwing a big holiday party)
- What benefits did you find in that imbalance?
- How do you find peace and enjoyment inside an imbalanced situation?
- Now that you know you can successfully deal with imbalance, how can you bring that peace and joy into the imbalance of everyday life?

Overcoming The Blahs
Why Making It About Others Might Just Help You Survive The Slump & Achieve Your Goals

Remember "sophomore slump?" The excitement of freshman year was long gone and road to graduation seemed almost infinite. Well, tonight I sit down to write the 13th chapter of what I hope will be a 50 chapter book (because 50 x my 2¢ = $1, which I think is hilarious — yes, I AM that much of a geek). And I have to admit, I might be suffering from the writer's version of the sophomore slump.

My mom and I were talking about this very thing the other day and wondering how I moved past my slump in The Penny Project. Certainly there had been one. Had I recognized it at the time? And without a "graduation" to look forward to, what kept me moving?

As with all my lessons learned from pennies, I once again found my answer in an unexpected way. This time, it happened to be a 12-part HBO miniseries about the Apollo space program.

If you've never seen it, you really should. It's called "From the Earth to the Moon" and spans the decade in which NASA dedicated itself to putting a man on the moon. More specifically, NASA put 12 men on the moon. But I'm betting most people reading this would only be able to name the first one.

Talk about the sophomore slump! The entire nation seemed to experience something like it after Apollo 11 successfully put Neil Armstrong and Buzz Aldrin on the moon. By the time Apollo 12 got up there, not many people were watching. Apparently, putting a 3rd and 4th man on the moon wasn't all that interesting.

Apollo 13 only got attention because something went wrong and they DIDN'T put men on the moon (gosh…I hope it's not the number 13 and this chapter is doomed too!).

The point is, as my mom and I talked about keeping the The Penny Project momentum going, we realized that even with really big, exciting projects (like putting men on the moon), people eventually lose interest.

And the truth is, if it had been just me, I probably would have given up on the pennies at some point. It was fun for a while. I learned some great lessons and drew a few interesting parallels between pennies and my life. But that only takes a girl so far. I was committed to collecting a year's worth of data, so I'm sure I would have completed at least one year. But what would have been the purpose of going on after that? Maybe I'd have done a second year to see if I could beat my record. But then what?

Thankfully, I wasn't the only penny collector out there. A few months into the first year, Illeny (my first official supporter) started bringing me her pennies, too.

I have to admit, the addition of a new person in my project threw me off a bit at first. My spreadsheet wasn't set up for multiple penny finders. I had to adjust the thing. It wasn't hard, but it was unexpected and gave me a new little jolt of energy around the project. Maybe change gets a bad wrap, and it isn't such a bad thing after all!

My next batch of supporters was also unexpected. What's more, their e-mails and texts reporting their findings brought me great (and unexpected) joy. Although I had come to find the task of collecting pennies fairly commonplace, here was a whole new group of folks sharing their excitement with me. My role turned from doer (finding the pennies) to motivator (encouraging OTHERS to find pennies).

That was the first shift that got me over my slump. It felt like magnified joy. A double shot of happiness — one for them and one for me!

As the months wore on, I saw other people wax and wane in their own penny finding journeys. I'd still get texts, but only if the coin was BIGGER than a penny. Then eventually, the texts would stop. But when one penny finder hung up her coin purse, another would pop into my life and I'd get excited all over again about sharing the experience with someone new.

I also found that each person brought a different energy to the project. Some involved their families. Nothing made me laugh like a text proclaiming someone's dad had spotted a dime and was sending it my way!

Others sent pictures of coins and bills they found.

A few people gave me penny art or wrote letters with pennies attached to brighten up my day. I really began to see the value of inviting others to share your passions — regardless of whether they are a little bizarre!

Even today, new penny finders always find their way into the picture. That's probably because I try to invite them when I can! Not only because I think others can benefit from some of the lessons I've learned, but because I benefit from the new energy they bring. Once I discovered the synergy of sharing, I was open to new things that would expand the project beyond what I had originally intended. What would be the next frontier? How many ways could I promote The Penny Project?

- A blog
- Fundraising (I partnered with a friend whose gala was themed "Pennies From Heaven")
- A documentary (which came to me through the blog)
- Monthly updates
- Working with a photojournalist
- Becoming a guest blogger on other sites to expand my audience

- Talking about it with my students in a way that would enhance their learning
- Donating the pennies to charity (which got us a mention on their website)

With each new project, I expanded my reach and renewed my excitement in pennies. And although there is no end in sight, I find I enjoy the journey as much today as I did when I started. I don't enjoy it in the SAME ways, but what in life really stays the same forever?

And in the long run, I'm glad I stuck with the pennies. Getting past the first year slump and keeping it going for others took me to a new level of learning. Some of the lessons I learned didn't ripen to perfection until recently. If I wasn't still tracking penny finds, those lessons may never have popped in my mind. I never would have hit $500, which was just the amount that the charity I donated it to needed. And I certainly wouldn't be writing my first book (a life-long dream of mine).

So by telling others about The Penny Project, they were able to remind me later of what's so great about it and why I should do it for another year. And then another…

It's kind of amazing and ironic all at once…sharing my passion with others led to THEIR enthusiasm, which kept my own alive.

Lesson

Share the light of your passion with others. You've got nothing to lose and everything to gain.

Think of your passion as a lighted candle. Everyone around you has a candle, too…only theirs aren't lit. As you share your flame with a few people, the room lights up! Your candle still burns brightly, but now all those whom you've touched have a light to share too. Not only are they now able to pass their light on to others, but when your candle blows out, they can pass the light back to you!

What are your 2 cents?

- What's the lighted candle you have burning in your soul?
- How can you share it with others?
- If you haven't shared it, what's stopping you?

Crafting Your Message

Why You Should Ask Yourself, "Do I Want To Do It My Way Or Achieve My Objectives?"

Long before I knew what I was going to do with the penny money, I was able to gather a number of supporters. Some people liked the challenge of finding money. Some were competitive and just wanted to stay in the lead on the spreadsheet. Others liked to be part of something bigger.

And then there was my student who just loved spreadsheets.

As The Penny Project began to develop, I found myself telling the story of how I got started over and over again. People really seemed to be amused by the story and often I'd get the question, "Does it have to be found money or can I just give you the change in my wallet?" Not one to turn down money for the cause (whatever it would turn out to be), my answer was always yes.

I said yes because, despite my lack of certainty about the precise way I'd use the money, I knew I loved collecting indiscriminate amounts and turning them into a meaningful chunk of change. I knew that the story of whatever this was turning into was fun to tell and even more fun to create as I went along.

And I knew, beyond a shadow of a doubt, that when the time came, I would know what to do with the money. So I kept collecting.

It wasn't like I had a predetermined amount in my head that I was trying to save. I was working with pennies, for heaven's sake. I was shocked to hit a dollar. And then I was shocked to hit ten. When I'd saved enough to open a savings account and earn interest, you could have knocked me over with a feather!

All I knew was my goal was to collect as much as I could by sharing my story. So I kept on gathering pennies.

While all of this was happening, I was continuing to live my life. Shocking, I know! It turns out that, even for me, there's more to life than just collecting pennies.

One of the things my job required me to do at the time was to get certified in a number of different psychometric tools. One of these tools, the DiSC assessment, was all about the different communication styles people preferred. The instructor of the course started out by walking us through how each of the styles operated. As he did, you could see the recognition on every participant's face as he spoke about each person's primary style of interacting.

The instructor gave examples of how each type might act, what a typical voicemail message would sound like, how the office of someone with this communication style would look, and other identifying style indicators. Members of the class began to chuckle when the instructor spoke of their types — you could see he was hitting the proverbial nail on the head.

After describing all of the types, the instructor then asked a very powerful question, "What do you think is the primary communication style of 90% of the population?"

Students began to shout out answers.

"D," said one man with certainty.

"Nope," answered the instructor.

"It's gotta be 'I'!" said someone else.

"Nope," replied the instructor again.

"C?" came another voice…this time a bit uncertain.

"Wrong again."

"Then I guess it's gotta be 'S,'" came the last reply, certainly right since the others had been ruled out.

"Actually," smiled the instructor as he was about to reveal the answer, "the correct answer is THEIR OWN. Most people communicate in their own style without regard to the preferred communication style of the person with whom they are communicating."

I thought this was fascinating! Looking around the room I could see that the people who'd said D, i, S, and C were those types themselves. Including me! I was certain that MY way of communicating HAD to be the way most people communicated. It just made good sense!

That course was a huge turning point for me and taught me a very important life lesson. Communication is not about saying what you want to say, it's about making sure the recipient hears the message you want them to hear. Big difference!

I left that course with a significantly increased awareness that not everyone was like me. It seems so obvious, but it's something I watch people ignore time and time again.

I've seen direct communicators bulldoze more indirect types. Or extroverts trample all over introverts. Sometimes analytical folks disregard the input of those who are more apt to follow a gut feeling. It's quite common to see people of all styles ignore or be put off by people who don't communicate the way THEY would communicate.

Since my mamma didn't raise no dummy, I took my newfound knowledge of this DiSC model and applied it to my co-workers. I realized my boss's boss was an analytical type who didn't like to be rushed in decision making matters. This was in direct opposition to my style of rolling with the punches and thinking on my feet. I recognized I needed to make some changes in my future interactions with her.

I began sending her agendas and information for our meetings several days before they actually took place. This allowed her to soak in all the data and think about it so she'd be ready to make decisions when we sat down face to face. She wasn't comfortable making decisions when she was hearing the information for the first time IN the meeting.

Even though it wasn't the way I personally preferred to communicate, I could see that by giving her the information and data ahead of time — not to mention the typed format versus the "trust me" conversations we'd been having — I was more apt to get the outcomes I wanted.

It became sort of fun to communicate with her because I felt like it was my own personal human laboratory experiment. I enjoyed figuring out the perfect way to deliver my message so I could get what I wanted. I was shocked at how often it actually worked! Maybe these psychometric tools were on to something!

Fast forward a year or so later to the student I mentioned previously who had a fondness for spreadsheets.

His colleagues had given him a bad time about it throughout the class and it had become somewhat of a running joke. One day, I decided to see if I could use that joke to connect with him about The Penny Project.

Unlike the story I told most people, which often prompted them to dig into their pockets for coins, I decided to try a different approach with my student.

It started a little something like this, "Hey Cary, I know how much you love spreadsheets…I want you to take a look at this one I whipped up for a project I'm doing."

From there, I shared a variation of my normal penny story. I focused heavily on the role of the spreadsheet by demonstrating all the different elements I tracked, the way I sorted the money by quarter (color coded, of course), and even the way an ex-boyfriend had enhanced it with embedded fiscal data and graphs!

He ate it up. In fact, he promptly got out his wallet and handed me a dollar. "I want you to add me to the spreadsheet," he said as he handed me the bill.

"Gladly," I smiled as I added his dollar to the donation column.

The smile wasn't just for the dollar (although that's a hundred pennies, so it was definitely something worth smiling about!). The smile was for the fact that I'd gotten what I wanted. I'd connected with my student and added a dollar to The Penny Project's bottom line. But he'd also gotten something he wanted — a rousing conversation about spreadsheets AND a chance to share ideas about possible enhancements for next year's tracking system.

Everybody wins.

Lesson

Whenever you enter a conversation in which you are seeking a specific outcome, you need to ask yourself, "Do I want to do it my way or do I want to achieve my objectives?" Whether you're trying to negotiate your salary or convince your spouse you want Mexican food instead of eating Italian yet again, you have to consider whether it's more important to communicate in your own style or to get the salary or cuisine you're after.

If you'd rather stick to your easygoing, go-with-the-flow way of doing things instead of adapting to the other person's direct, get-it-done-now style, that's ok. Just be aware that this choice might come with a less attractive dollar amount or another plate of spaghetti.

The next time you have to approach a conversation with someone you typically have a hard time communicating with, consider these questions:

- What is YOUR primary communication style?
- How does it differ from the person you have a hard time communicating with?
- What changes could you make to the way you approach conversations with that person to be a little closer to his/her style rather than your own?
- And most importantly, is getting what you REALLY want worth making those changes?

What are your 2 cents?

- Think about a specific experience in which you lost out on your main objective because the person you were talking to didn't like your communication style. How could you approach it differently to create a more desirable outcome?

- Conversely, think about a specific experience in which you got what you wanted simply because you adapted the way you communicated to someone else's style. What lessons or tricks did you learn from this success?
- How can you strive to understand the needs of those with whom you are communicating in order to facilitate a win-win solution?

Leadership
Why Leadership Isn't A One Size Fits All Kind Of Thing

Aside from pennies, my other true love is leadership. Having spent four years at West Point, I studied, watched, and practiced what it means to be a good leader. Not that I'm perfect by any means, but the opportunities I've had to lead people have been some of the best times of my life.

To me, there is nothing better than watching a good leader in action. It gives me goose bumps.

Conversely, bad leadership hurts my head AND my heart. But I don't like to think about what I don't like to think about. So let's focus on what makes a good leader.

A good leader encompasses a number of qualities, such as caring, compassion, competence, commitment and a whole bunch of other words that may or may not begin with 'C'. But one of the most important things a leader does is inspire people.

Just like I mentioned the different ways people communicate, inspiration runs along those same lines. A leader's job isn't to figure out how to inspire "the team" by coming up with one systematic approach that works for everyone. A leader's job is to figure out how to inspire individuals by learning what it is that gets each and every one of them motivated. This might include recognition, increased responsibility, a private, heartfelt thank you, or a more public reward presented in front of the individual's peers.

The question isn't about what inspires YOU, it's about what inspires THEM. Don't assume you know unless you ask.

OK…even though I said I didn't want to talk about bad leadership, I do want to mention one valuable lesson I learned when I focused too much on one so-called "bad leader" from my past.

The last job I had before I began working for myself was a pretty good one. Or at least it WAS a good one before we got restructured and my boss got a new boss. I was convinced that woman was the devil incarnate. She was everything I strived not to be as a leader. She was cold, unreceptive, and heard to have said some pretty nasty things about my boss (whom I loved). And those were her good qualities.

Working for her was like having a rock in my shoe that I couldn't figure out how to remove, annoying to say the least. This dynamic created a constant, ongoing conversation with my life coach. I couldn't stand the woman and continuously told him how much it galled me that SHE actually got to lead people. Life was unfair.

During one of our calls, I was ranting and raving about how awful she was and how she'd said such nasty things about people. My coach waited until I came up for air and calmly asked, "You know those people who have to tear others down to feel better about themselves?"

"Yes," I replied, thinking that's exactly the kind of person she was. "I hate those people."

"Well, that's what you're doing to this woman in your head," he continued.

The statement hit me like a ton of bricks.

"What?" I couldn't believe what I had just heard. How did I suddenly become the villain here?

"You know how you're always saying how much you love leadership and that you want the opportunity to be a leader? Well it seems to me you're just tearing her down in your head so you can feel like the good leader you want to be. If she's the 'BAD' leader in your story, then you get to be the 'GOOD' leader by default."

Was my coach right? Had I become one of those people I hated, tearing someone else down so I could feel better about myself? Even if I was only doing it in my head (which clearly I wasn't since he just called me on it), that's no good.

As a million thoughts went through my mind, my coach continued, "Instead of complaining about the bad leadership you see, why don't you just BE a good leader?"

I had a bunch of reasons that wouldn't work. I didn't have a staff. The company was crazy. I didn't even care about the mission that much.

He called me on all of it. "Just be a leader. In whatever capacity you can. Create the environment you want to lead in and then lead. It's that simple."

If only it was. I got off the phone feeling like a negative ninny who probably couldn't (or shouldn't) try to lead herself after that nasty conversation, let alone anyone else. Perhaps I needed to rethink what it means to be a leader.

Fortunately, going out on my own allowed me to do just that. As a facilitator, I knew I didn't have the authority to make decisions. And though I couldn't tell the organizations I worked with what to do, they often looked to me for guidance. Even though my role and title didn't indicate it, I felt like a leader.

It wasn't until later that I realized leadership is also part of what The Penny Project had become for me — my own little world where I got to be the kind of leader I would want to follow.

Sure, my impact on any of the people who've contributed to the project isn't the same as if I was their supervisor or boss. But doesn't that make it even more challenging? I have no control over them. Their participation is completely voluntary.

And I have to figure out what motivates each of the people who contribute. At least that's what I have to do if I want them to KEEP contributing!

• Some want recognition in the quarterly updates.

- Some want to be in the lead on the spreadsheet and are motivated by competition.
- Some prefer a handwritten note of thanks for their donations.
- Some don't care a flip about pennies but know the project is important to me.
- Some want me to share their funny stories on the blog.
- Some want to be involved in decisions…like, should we accept found FOREIGN money?
- Some don't want to be motivated — they're one time givers and that's OK too!!

I remember one friend in particular who wasn't going to be convinced, cajoled, or coerced into picking up pennies.

Stephanie was a bit of a skeptic about the whole "picking up pennies from the ground" thing. It wasn't her cup of tea, which I understood (especially given some of the crazy situations I've found myself in while hunting for a few cents). And even if she did find one, she certainly wasn't going to pick it up if it was "tails up." That's just asking for a dose of bad luck! Stephanie is also, as you might have guessed, a bit "superstitious."

But the tide turned one day when she went to dinner with her mom (a very beautiful and elegant woman) who put a penny on the table and said, "Give this to Leslie."

A few days later, we were at our favorite Happy Hour spot after work when Steph sauntered back from the restroom, placed a penny on the bar and said, "Here...I don't know what you do with these, but I found it on the sink in the restroom." And so began Steph's participation in The Penny Project!

Who would have guessed that just a few months later she'd have a dime's worth of pennies on the spreadsheet and a story from her new job about love, balance, and how superstitions might have exceptions?

Leslie,

I found not ONE, but TWO pennies yesterday. Where, you ask?

One was outside (heads up) next to the wedding I was shadowing for work. The ACTUAL wedding (you know, bride, groom, priest, et al.). The other was inside (tails up) at their reception/dinner.

I think it is an omen to find two pennies at a WEDDING, both on different sides up...they complete one another!!! Just like the bride and groom. :-)

Awww....

This was such a great story that I asked Steph if I could share it on my blog, which she was happy to let me do. A blogger herself, being recognized for her clever heads/tails interpretation was a good motivator. Certainly much more effective than saying, "You're falling behind on the spreadsheet!" Although this method works beautifully for some, it wouldn't have done the trick to get Steph on board.

Since that incident, Steph has gone on to find another quarter's worth of pennies because she discovered a way to find the positive side of a tails up penny. Something she wouldn't have tried to do if I'd foo-fooed her superstition in the first place.

In the end, as the leader of this project, with a growing vision of where I want it to go, it's my job to inspire and encourage people to contribute in ways that works for them. It doesn't matter if those ways work for me or for any of the other penny collectors. As long as I can find a way to connect with each individual and inspire them accordingly, the pennies just seem to keep rolling in!

Lesson

Leadership is a gift...and a privilege. When you get the opportunity to lead others, spend some time figuring out how you can inspire them.

- Do they prefer public or private recognition?
- What kind of rewards would make them feel valued?
- How do they feel connected to the project you're working on?

If you can find these things out early on, you'll be more apt to tailor your approach to each individual in a way that will work for them. And when your team is happy because they feel you're taking care of them, they'll want to return the favor. And when a team creates that kind of synergy, there are no bounds on what you can achieve together!

What are your 2 cents?

- How are you best motivated? Do you need to be challenged, rewarded, or pressured, to name a few?
- When was the last time you received recognition for something you did, and did you like the way you were commended for your work? If not, how would you have preferred to be recognized?
- Who has been the most inspirational or effective leader in your life? Why?

Persistence
Why Just Showing Up
Is Sometimes Half The Battle

I was recently asked to recount the story of my adventures in trapeze school. Although you might think I'm a bit of a clown, I'm actually more of a flying art-eest (pronounced in the snooty French way).

I had always heard about taking trapeze lessons and hoped to someday get the opportunity to give it a try. So it was a no-brainer when I started planning a trip to the Bahamas and found out one of the resorts had a trapeze school on-site. The place was all-inclusive, which meant I could fly through the air with the greatest of ease to my little heart's content.

On the first full day at the resort, I went to the trapeze training area to get the skinny. I learned about the required attire and schedule for the lessons. That was all I needed to know to sign up. I was in!

I showed up for my first lesson ready and raring to go. I got introductory instructions and practice time on a low-hanging trapeze. This only lasted a few minutes before I was sent over to get my harness. It was not the most comfortable thing to wear, but I was still excited to put it on because it meant I was one step closer to my first attempt at flying!

I waited in line and watched the people before me perform their tricks with grace. There were a number of options for preparing to release the bar in an attempt to do "the catch," which is when one of the professional flyers grabs you mid-air after your release.

The main trick, and the one I'd be attempting first, was called the "knee hang." To get into the proper position, I'd start out hanging from the bar by my hands. On the first swing out, I'd tuck my knees into my chest and hook my feet on the bar. On the second swing out, I'd hang completely upside down and reach behind me to simulate reaching for the catch. After that, I'd un-tuck, hang straight, and drop into the safety net.

As I waited, I watched trick after trick go off without a hitch. One teenage girl did a fancy trick with a split and got wild applause from the onlookers. It all looked pretty easy and I was excited to get up on the platform!

When it was my turn, I climbed up the narrow ladder, which I figured would probably be harder than the trick itself. I was hooked in and the team member on the ground was going to instruct me on when to jump. I waited for the call and when the time came, I leapt off the platform…like a ton of bricks.

I think I might have even screamed a little. I wasn't scared, just totally surprised at how the whole thing felt. It was not at all what I expected.

I had been so thrown off by the feeling; I couldn't even get myself positioned to hang from my knees on the bar, which was the main objective.

No worries. The instructors told me to dismount and just give it another try.

I hit the net, climbed down, and got back in line to get a "do over."

The second time, since I knew what to expect, I was ready to tuck into position when I jumped off the platform. But for some reason, my tucking skills weren't so good and I blew my timing.

Again, the instructors told me it was no big deal and to try it again.

They also said that on my 3rd attempt, and again on my 4th.

By the time I'd tried to get a well-timed knee hang five times, the lessons were over for the day and I was not approved to move on to the next stage, which was attempting a catch. My timing just wasn't good enough to get a shot at working with the professionals.

I was a little bummed I didn't get to try the catch, but knew I'd be back the next day to try my trick again. I stayed to watch the other flyers do their catches. Some made them, some didn't, but all of them were neat to watch and I enjoyed cheering on my fellow, wannabe trapeze artists!

I did indeed come back the next day and give the old knee hang another try. Again, I had the same timing problems I'd had on the first day. The instructors shouted out instructions trying to be helpful, but I just didn't have the flexibility I needed to tuck my body into a knee hang. I was really starting to get flustered. Not to mention, my legs were bruised up and down from my repeated attempts to get the timing right.

Seeing the frustration on my face, one of the instructors pulled me aside and told me there was another way to do the knee hang. Although 99% of people had no problem with the tuck (not exactly what I needed to hear), there was another way to get into the same position to attempt the catch. She told me that instead of tucking, I could bring my legs all the way around the outside of the bar (sort of a spread-eagle looking movement) and hook my legs OUTSIDE my hands.

I gave it a try on the practice bar and seemed to have much less trouble getting into that position. I tried it again and again and had no problems. So I figured I'd give it a try on the real trapeze.

I got back in line behind a girl who I'd seen do tricks the past two days. She was REALLY good. I felt a bit sheepish coming up for my umpteenth try after so many unsuccessful attempts. She was clearly advanced and could do things way beyond the basic trick I was still trying to learn.

She must've seen me trying to do the alternate knee hang on the low bar because when I sat down next to her she said, "Don't feel bad. I couldn't get the regular knee hang my first time either. They taught me the way she just showed you. It's much easier — worked like a charm for me!"

I couldn't believe it. This girl, who was so good they'd asked her to be in that night's special trapeze show starring resort guests, had had trouble with the knee hang, too! Not that I like to hear about other people suffering, but I did feel better knowing that at one point, she was one of the other 1% of people who couldn't tuck!

She went on to tell me that the whole reason she'd come back to this resort again was to conquer that damn knee tuck! Turns out a little time away had done her good. Not only was she a seemingly skilled guest flyer, but they'd asked her to stay on for two weeks as part of the crew while one of the other girls went on vacation. She said she'd always wanted to run off and join the circus — what better way to live that dream than two weeks as a trapeze instructor/performer on an island in the Bahamas! She was my idol!

It was finally my turn to go and I made my way once again to the ladder. The staff and other guests were all cheering for me as I waited to see if this method would be the one that would work. I jumped off the platform when the instructor called the command. Forward, split, hook the legs, lie back, and reach. I did it! My timing had been perfect using this new technique!

The instructors wanted me to try it one more time before they okayed me to try the catch that afternoon (to make sure it wasn't a lucky fluke, I suppose). So I did. And again, it was perfect!

I hung around until it was time for the catch. I was stoked!!

Each guest gets two attempts to do a catch, which has two parts. First, you release your bar and the professional trapeze artist catches you. Then as you swing back towards your bar, you push off of his arms, twist, and try to catch your own bar as it swings toward you. It's pretty cool to see when someone gets it all to work.

Before I knew it, my first chance for the catch had arrived. Just as I had with the practice tricks, I jumped on command and hooked my knees without a hitch. When I reached back to grab the hands of the professional flyer, he was RIGHT THERE! He caught me! It was awesome — a total rush!

But in a split second the exhilaration passed and it was time to focus on the return. Once again I had to tune in and listen to the commands from the staff and release when the bar was coming back my way. I let go when she told me to, twisted, reached, and fell flat on my ass in the safety net. No joy on the return.

I was still pretty stoked that the first part of the catch had worked and was excited that I got one more try. Well…excited, but sore. All those practices had left my poor, bruised legs hurting quite a bit. One more trick was about all I had in me on that day.

Tired, but satisfied with my progress, I once again climbed the ladder. Perhaps it was all the bruises or maybe it was my sore arms and shoulders from two days of swinging like a monkey, but this time I didn't connect on the first part of the catch and fell right into the net. The instructors were still really nice about it and told me they were sure I'd get it tomorrow! I think they'd been surprised I came back after my rough first day. I'd taken quite a beating and clearly didn't have any NATURAL talent for this!

But it was fun. And I like a good challenge! I hoped they were right that I'd get it the next day. It was my last full day at the resort and my final chance to nail the trick!

My friend Illeny had made this trip with me and, thus far, I'd been unable to convince her she should come try the trapeze with me. She was more interested in snorkeling and wasn't all that excited about the idea of jumping off a platform 30 feet up in the air, even if she was connected to a harness. I kept talking about it all through dinner and got her to at least consider joining me for our last chance to fly.

We woke up the next day and all I could think about were my sore legs. Wow, those bars are rough on the old knees! Despite the bruising and soreness, I would not be deterred from my mission. I WOULD complete a full catch today!

When the time came for that day's lessons, it was a bit too breezy to enjoy snorkeling, so Illeny came with me to check out the trapeze school. I'd opted to practice only once that day and save the rest of my energy for the catch.

Being new, Illeny had to get the full rundown and prove she'd be good enough to do the catch. She was apparently a circus performer in a previous life because she nailed it on her first try and they said she only had to practice again if she really wanted to. She was approved for the catch.

I'm not one for a battle of egos, but I was a bit deflated by Illeny's immediate success in this endeavor. Especially since I'd been beating myself up for two days and had the bruises to prove it. Nonetheless, I HAD begged her to join me, so I was happy she thought it was as much fun as I'd promised.

When the time came to do the catch, Illeny preceded me so I could video tape her with my camera (and then instruct her how to do the same for me, because I was GOING to get this!). She climbed the ladder, took her position, and proceeded to totally nail her first ever catch.

Crap.

Not that her success in any way diminished my experience, but it was a bit frustrating to watch someone walk in and easily do something I'd been trying to do for three days. I suddenly felt some serious competitive pressure to succeed.

Illeny dismounted the net and was stoked about her awesome performance. I don't blame her, I'd have been stoked, too. I know how hard it is!

After she un-harnessed, I showed her how to work the video setting on my camera and then headed to the ladder.

I took a deep breath, waited for the command and then jumped off the platform. I did everything on cue, but like I had the day before, I missed the return.

Not a huge deal. I still had one more try.

Illeny took her second turn and did another great catch, although this time she too missed the return. It was getting a bit breezy and they had the smallest woman on the crew working the safety lines, which provide some of the momentum that helps the bar swing back to you for the return. All in all, Illeny was happy with her trapeze experience. After all, she was a natural and nailed her first catch!

I once again handed her my camera and headed for the ladder. I felt like I wasn't the only one who wanted to see me succeed here. The staff had put a considerable amount of time into giving me pointers and helping me improve. I felt like they were rooting for me. I'd also made friends with some of the other guests, who also wanted to see me nail this sucker!

So, with loads of support and a strong will to succeed, I climbed up to the platform.

I waited for the command and when it came…I JUMPED!! I swung forward, hooked my legs, swung back, and released my hands. I swung forward again, reached for the pro and…CONNECTION!! Jerome had a firm grip on me, one I could easily push off of for the return. We swung forward, and on the way back (on cue from the girl on the safety ropes), I pushed off and reached back for the bar… reaching, reaching, reaching…and then falling, falling, falling… right into the net. I'd missed my last chance for a full catch.

I was more than a little bummed. I felt that of all of my attempts, this had definitely been the best. I wasn't sure why I hadn't been able to grab the bar on the return. All of this ran through my head as I laid there in the net for a second. But there was no need to mope. The whole experience had been a completely fantastic adventure. How many people can say they've done trapeze tricks with trained professionals? I had nothing to complain about.

As I rolled over and made my way to the edge of the net to dismount, I heard a bit of a buzz between two of the instructors. As I dismounted and started to unbuckle my harness, they told me to hold on just a second.

Even though it was late in the day and we were out of time for attempting any more catches, they wanted to give me one last chance. It turns out that the reason I missed the return on that final attempt had something to do with the safety ropes not being pulled hard enough to give the bar the momentum it needed to fight the breeze. What they wanted to do was bring out their biggest guy to work the ropes so that I had every advantage on this last attempt.

I was all at once excited and a little emotional. It was really nice of them to give me this extra chance. I knew they were tired and had other things they could be doing, so it meant a lot that they would, as a team, pull together to put the best people in all the right places to help me successfully do a catch.

So, for the really, REALLY last time, I climbed the ladder to the platform. I waited for my command and took my final leap. On my end, it couldn't have gone any smoother. I'd mastered that pesky knee hang using the alternate technique they showed me. When I reached back to connect with Jerome, he was right there! I unhooked my legs and swung with him away from my bar.

Now it was time for the moment of truth. Would this final chance be what I needed to complete the catch? Dennis, the big guy they'd brought in to work the safety ropes, called out for me to release and turn back to my bar. I pushed off Jerome's arms and turned to see the bar out of the corner of my eye. I reached up to grab it and felt it slip out of the fingers on my right hand.

But I wasn't going to let that be the end of the story…so I reached juuuuust a little further with my left hand. And, wouldn't you know it, I caught a piece of that bar! I caught enough of it that I hung on and was able to reach up and grab it with my right hand, too.

It wasn't the prettiest return ever done, but it was mine!

I crossed hand over hand, turned to face Jerome and then did a back-flip dismount off the bar to what felt like wild applause from the ground.

Catch complete. Mission accomplished!

Those three days at the resort remind me a lot of the three years I've been doing The Penny Project. What links these two experiences is that no matter what happens, I just keep showing up.

To the amazement of the staff at the resort, I didn't let a lack of skill or numerous failed attempts keep me from continuing to pursue my goal of being able to complete a catch. Likewise, to the amazement of people I tell about The Penny Project, I don't let a lack of direction or unknown outcome prevent me from continuing to pick up pennies in pursuit of…well…something.

I have learned the invaluable lesson of persistence — of not giving up. I did it during my three days at the resort, which I'm pretty sure is why they granted me that final try so I could do a successful catch. I also do it every day with the pennies. I've had some setbacks (naysayers, lost data on the spreadsheets, dry spells) but don't let them stop me from continuing to follow the pennies where they take me.

And as I've followed that path, the destination has become clearer and clearer.

Sometimes, it's just about showing up and being willing to see where the road's gonna take you today.

Lesson

Attendance is half the battle. There were a few classes I passed in college just because I'd been there to hear what the professor said and could repeat those words back to him on an exam. I'll admit now I never did a single reading assignment in my military history class. I also never missed a day. I knew I could pass just by writing down what I heard every day during the lectures.

Showing up makes a difference. Whatever goals you set for yourself in life, show up in some small way every day to achieve them. You have to be there to reach your goals. Not a thing gets reached when you're not trying.

If I'd skipped the second day of trapeze practice, no one would have been interested in making sure I got an extra try on the third day.

And if I'd stopped picking up pennies after a few months, I never would've found more than the $20 that motivated me to start the project. I'd have missed some pretty valuable life lessons. There wouldn't have been much of a story to write about on the blog, which wouldn't have been found by guys looking for a "pro-penny" interviewee for their penny movie. My persistence was rewarded with the pennies I kept finding and confirmed by spreadsheets full of data. Even when I had no idea what the outcome would be!

What are your 2 cents?

- What are the things in life you REALLY want?
- How do you make a habit of showing up? Or, not showing up, if that is the case?
- If you repeated today 365 times, would you be closer to your goals a year from now?

Giving Your Pennies Away

Why Despite The Excitement Of Big Gifts, The Best Things Really Do Come In Small Packages

After two and half years of picking up pennies, sharing my story and collecting money from other people for a bigger cause (despite not actually knowing what that bigger cause was), I finally found a way to give away my pennies.

Or more accurately, someone asked for my pennies.

It had long been the dream of my friend Erica to put on a conference dedicated to helping young women between the ages of 14-17 build self-esteem. She'd read studies showing that was the age range when boys' self-esteem increased, while girls of the same age range showed a decrease in their self-esteem.

For the inaugural Young Women's National Conference (YWNC), an event filled with workshops and panels to help promote "girl power" by reinforcing the self esteem of young girls in that 14-17 year old age range, Erica asked if I wanted to be a board member for the conference. As such, I could influence the content and make sure one of the panels available would be about financial literacy, something with which The Penny Project could be associated.

I was honored to be asked, especially since this was Erica's dream! What a special experience to work with someone who has the passion to create and produce a new event dedicated to such a worthy cause.

I agreed to be on the board, although I wasn't exactly sure what that meant. In the early stages of The Penny Project, my friend and superb penny finder Michele and I talked about creating a Penny Board. Well versed in board life, she told me members generally had three choices — "give, get, or get off." As in, give money, get donors, or get the hell off the board!

I wasn't sure which category I'd fill, but I figured at the very least I would support Erica however I could to make sure her dream became a reality.

One way I knew I could do that was to share my pennies. After all, I'd been collecting them with the intention of giving them to a good cause. And what better cause was there than helping a friend achieve a dream that was all about helping other people?

So, I told Erica I wanted to be a sponsor and donate $500 of my penny money to the conference.

She was very thankful and excited to have a sponsor. I knew $500 was only a drop in the bucket of what we needed, but I was excited to finally have someplace to donate the pennies so I could report back to my dedicated penny finders about the cause their hard earned (ok, hard FOUND) pennies would be supporting.

In addition to donating money, I also agreed to lead the financial literacy panel. This meant I had to find people to speak on the panel, determine content and questions, and make sure the overall session kept the girls' attention. Although I'm a pro at adult classes, I had my work cut out for me figuring out how to keep teenage girls engaged for 90 minutes.

The money and helping to organize the panel certainly helped me check the "give" block on the "good board member" checklist. I was also going to seek out other, bigger donors (such as corporate sponsors for the financial literacy panel). But I still wanted to do more to ensure the success of the event.

I decided to talk to some of the other women I knew who owned small businesses that might want to donate or be part of the conference. My friend Jenn, a fitness expert who specializes in training young women in youth sports, decided not only to be a sponsor, but she also volunteered to lead a mid-morning fitness break where the girls would learn some exercise tips and health-related information.

I was pretty sure this meant I could also check off the "get" block on my board member to-do list!

As with any project, planning and organizing the YWNC saw plenty of ups and downs over the months we worked on it. Trying to organize so many busy women was a big challenge. Scheduling meetings everyone could attend was next to impossible. Some board members were fairly active, while others seemed to be on the board in name only. I figured these were what Michele meant when she told me about the "get off" category.

I did what I could, but being in the midst of my first full year as a small business owner, my availability was pretty scarce as well.

As we drew closer to the day of the event, registration numbers weren't where we needed them to be. Erica held a quick call with the board to let us know we needed to have 50 girls registered by the end of the week or the company sponsoring the venue was going to pull their support. This meant we each needed to register two girls to meet the quota.

Although I'd been as helpful as I could with donations and finding sponsors, I didn't have ready access to an audience of 14-17 year old girls. My best bet was my sister's soon-to-be step daughter. I called and offered to pay to register her and a friend for the event, but found out their homecoming was the weekend of the conference.

No dice.

Not happy that I'd failed my mission in regards to improving our registration numbers, I called to let Erica know I hadn't been able to register my two.

I also wanted to see how she was holding up now that we were down to the final days before the event. In addition to the planning, scrambling, and fighting for registrants (she literally went to high school football games and other teen-drawing venues to hand out flyers and talk up the event), her husband was laid off from his job.

Talk about bad timing.

Although she was certainly concerned about the event's success and had lots of other things on her mind, talking with Erica and providing the best moral support I could seemed to help. She said that often times throughout the previous months, my checking in on the things I'd done had really helped to lift her spirits and reenergize her to make sure this event actually happened!

That was certainly nice to hear, but I couldn't help but think I should have done more. Unfortunately, the conference happened to fall smack dab in the middle of my busiest month of the year. So at some point, I just had to let go and know I'd done all I physically could to help Erica make the event a success.

The day of the event I showed up and have to say I was completely wowed by what she had put together. Everything from the signage to the food looked totally professional and was definitely something she could be proud of. Attendance turned out better than we had hoped with over 85 girls participating, 35 speakers and panelists, and 25 additional mentors and support staff.

I was so thrilled to see Erica's dream become a reality in front of our very eyes. She was so positive — she even said that it had been somewhat of a blessing that Sean, her husband, was free to help out so much at the end. He was responsible for all the beautiful signs, program certificates, and other printed materials we used throughout the day. Talk about seeing the glass half full!

As the experience wound down and I reflected on the part I had played in making it happen, I realized I'd actually done a lot I could be proud of. Sure, there were things I didn't do (I never did find a corporate sponsor for my financial literacy panel), but since the money I'd donated came from The Penny Project, I tried to look at it all though my penny perspective.

Although I had really wanted to deliver big things to Erica (like a corporate sponsor), I was happy with the little ways I helped her out. While the big things would have been the equivalent of handing her a $20 bill, each small thing was a penny, and those pennies added up. More than once, she said how thankful she was to have had me on the board. She also thanked me numerous times both privately and publically saying she couldn't have done it without me, mentioning both my financial and emotional support.

So, in the end, I learned a lot from this process, as well. And the biggest lesson of all? While $20 bills are nice, the pennies we collect really do add up!

Lesson

Don't get caught in the "bigger is better" trap when it comes to giving back. Whether you are giving to a cause or helping out a friend, grand gestures aren't required to show someone how much you care.

While we all love the idea of someone swooping in to save the day (or for some of us, BEING the person who swoops in and saves the day), there's something to be said for the people in our lives who offer us constant support in a dozen little ways.

- The friend who motivates us to go to the gym.
- The neighbor who cooks us dinner when she knows we've got nothing in the fridge.
- The co-worker who knows just when to send a funny e-mail to make the day stop dragging by.
- The sister who calls five times a day just to say hi and see what you had for lunch.

None of the ways these people support us is life-changing, much like finding a penny won't make you rich. But the sum total is one that provides way more value than a one-time "swoop in and save the day" move.

So the next time someone you know needs help and the task seems like more than you can handle, take a look inside and see what penny-sized support you have to offer.

What are your 2 cents?

- In what small ways can you show a friend that you support what he or she is doing?
- How can you give back to your community without draining your wallet or yourself?
- What constant support in your life has been meaningful, and how can you "pay it forward?"

Life Being Easy

Why Sometimes, Despite Our Best Efforts To Complicate Things, They Really ARE That Easy

Some of my best ideas of all time come to me while I'm on vacation. Maybe it's because I'm not working too hard. Or maybe it's because I've worked so hard BEFORE the vacation that my brain finally gets to process what's inside.

Whatever the case, I realized during one holiday that sometimes things don't have to be as hard as we make them. Not even when it comes to finding pennies.

I was visiting Hawaii with two of my best girlfriends. They are the kind of girls who will run screaming to beat you to a penny (I know this because we did it once while walking around Washington, DC clamoring like magpies every time we found one…it was SO much fun!).

One day while I was alone at the hotel pool, I decided to take a dip in the water. I bookmarked my trashy novel, took off my cover-up, and walked over to the edge of the pool.

I walked all the way down the steps into the water to cool off in the summer heat. After I'd cooled off a bit, I found a spot on the edge of the pool and just dangled my feet in the water.

As I sat there, appreciating the fact my friend Jenn had been generous enough to invite Misty and I to join her on this work trip, I looked up at the beautiful palm trees that surrounded the pool. When I looked back down, I noticed a pool floatie (a bright orange inner tube) was sort of floating my way. It was unattended and didn't appear to belong to anyone.

As it got closer, I squinted to see if I was really seeing what I thought I saw.

Sure enough, on the edge of the inner tube closest to me, sitting there, as if it was guiding the tube in my direction, was a bright, shiny dime.

Now, I'm not one to look a gift dime in the mouth, but what the hell was this all about?!

I thought for sure one of my friends had played a joke on me and set that dime there for me to find. But Jenn was at her conference and Misty had gone for a run. I looked around at the faces of the people around the pool. Clearly no one realized the significance of this dime. And no one was laughing or pointing, a pretty good sign my friends hadn't just played a good joke on me.

Next, I thought the dime must've belonged to some kid or the family this floatie belonged to. Again, I scanned the pool for a look or maybe an angry glare as if to say, "Mitts off our floatie AND our dime!"

Again…I saw nothing.

Was it possible that I had just scored the world's easiest money find? While on vacation, in Hawaii, had a dime really just floated right up to me as if to send the message, "Yes, Leslie, there is a Santa Clause"?

I was in a state of total bliss. THIS was too good not to share!

Normally, when it comes to anything in my life I want to share, my mom is the first person I call. But when it comes to penny stories, I can't help but dial my dad first and tell him about the funny (or sometimes strange) things that happen to me.

I called to tell him about the dime on the floatie and we both got a good laugh!

"Dad, the funny thing is, I was just having an experience this morning where I had the same thought…is life REALLY this easy? "

I excitedly went on to relay the story. "A girl I know from school e-mailed me out of the blue and offered to help me do some content development for a project I'm working on. She said she wasn't sure what had made her write or if I even needed her help, but I do need her help! I just kept reading the message thinking, it can't be this easy to get help on a project right when I need it! But maybe, just maybe, it really IS that easy!"

We chatted for a while about how sometimes there really are things in life that come just at the right time or seem to be a perfect fit. We also laughed about how we often talk ourselves out of such easiness thinking, "Surely if it's that easy, it's no good!"

It was a great conversation and, after a few minutes, I told him I should probably go hang out by the pool and see what other great revelations (and money) would come to me!

As I headed back to the pool's edge, I couldn't help but think about how easy my life had felt lately. In fact, the trip I was on had fallen into place with ridiculous ease. The plane ticket had cost just $5 (thanks to my obsession with frequent flier miles). The hotel was free (thanks to Jenn's conference and then Misty's hotel points). And my schedule had just opened up so I could take the week off for the trip.

Perhaps all of that ease was so I could sit poolside, have a dime float right up to me, and finally see that, yes, sometimes life IS just that easy!

Sometimes the only easy thing about life is talking ourselves out of things that come to us without a struggle.

Our inner saboteur tells us, "You didn't work hard enough to deserve that." Or "It must not be any good if it was that easy to get."

Lesson

But sometimes — and I'd even venture to say OFTEN times — when we're doing what we love, paying attention to how the little things in life make us feel, and just enjoying the journey we're on, that's exactly when things become easy!

I can tell you that nothing was easier than just going with the flow and accepting my friends' invitation to Hawaii. Less than $200 spent for the entire week with great friends in a paradise-like setting, and getting a tan to boot!

Not to mention getting a floatie-dime life lesson, of course.

So the next time you stumble upon some incredible good luck or things seem to be going your way, don't let those voices in your head talk you out of knowing you deserve it.

Just like knowing each penny has value, so too do our "easy" experiences in life. Maybe they're easy because we've laid the right ground work and are exactly where we're supposed to be in our journeys.

Now's the time to silence your inner saboteur and rewrite the story you tell yourself when things come easy!

What are your 2 cents?

- What is your saboteur's version of "easy can't be good?"
- What easy experiences in your life have you discounted as not being valuable?
- What easy experience in your life have you recognized as being invaluable?

Sharing Your Dreams

Why Letting Everyone Know What You Want Makes Sense Because They Might Be The Ones To Give It To You

My life got infinitely more interesting the day I decided to start my own business. I did it more as a tax precaution than anything else. I was doing some consulting work on the side and my accountant told me I'd need to incorporate my freelance business to keep more of the money I was making. And if anyone wants to keep more of the money she's making, it's a girl who picks up pennies out of the gutter!

So I became the accidental business owner. I still had a full time job, but occasionally did work on the side as a facilitator and trainer.

That is, until I got laid off. Then all of a sudden I wasn't doing anything on the side anymore. The company I'd founded became front and center in my life.

At first, I wasn't sure what to tell people. Was I looking for a replacement job or did I want to keep doing consulting work? Was I a project manager (since most people knew what that meant) or did I want to focus on facilitation (which meant fighting the uphill battle of explaining what I do to everyone)?

I opted to try out the self-employed route for a while and see where it led me.

Much like The Penny Project, I had no idea where it would go. What I did know was that I enjoyed facilitating groups and from what I'd experienced so far, I was pretty good at it. I decided to start letting people know I was on my own now and interested in work as a facilitator and trainer.

Not long after being laid off, I began taking classes to become certified as a life coach. During the five months I was in those classes, I became close to several of the other women in my group. During breaks we'd talk about what we did when we weren't coaching, which of course for me meant letting people know I was newly self-employed and building my business as a facilitator.

The more I talked about it, the more support I got. Words of encouragement, ideas on how to generate leads, and even a few serious work offers for the coming months started flowing my way. One of the jobs actually panned out and was the bulk of my income for a three month period. All of these positive developments happened because I was willing to chatter on excitedly about how much I love facilitation. Turns out, my energy was a bit contagious and just what people are looking for in a facilitator!

It reminds me so much of the way The Penny Project grew.

After gaining my first few supporters (my friends Illeny and Michele were certain this was an idea that would catch on), I couldn't help myself from talking about the fun we were having with pennies. At first, I just shared my stories with friends and family. But as time wore on, any pair of ears looked like a good opportunity for me to mention pennies!

One day it struck me that not only had I shaped my environment by talking about the pennies, but I'd also influenced the people WITHIN my environment. The sum total was a state of never-ending, unfailing penny finding.

I happened to be visiting my on-again, off-again boyfriend, Ryan, in San Francisco when this flash of brilliance hit me. Although we were a bit of a disaster when it came to dating, he was a very supportive penny finder! I even got picture texts when he found multiple pennies at one time. He clearly had a good eye!

We were walking around Fisherman's Wharf one day and, as usual, I was darting in and out of crowds grabbing pennies from under people's feet as we walked past counter after counter of clam chowder sellers. We eventually stopped to get our own chowder and ate it as we watched the seagulls and tourists go — and sometimes fly — by.

When we were done, we continued wandering around the piers. As we walked, I was blabbing on about something when Ryan suddenly grabbed my shoulders and physically turned me to see a PILE of pennies in a doorway we were about to pass.

"I don't understand how you can see one penny under a guy's shoe, but miss an entire pile of pennies in a doorway."

It was a fair question. "I was talking?" I replied sheepishly. Admittedly, I did do about 80% of the talking when we were together, so he sort of laughed and looked at me as if to express the sentiment, 'you don't say.'

"Besides," I went on, "I was looking at you and facing the street. You were looking at me and facing the doorway where all the pennies were lying. Either way, they're found and will be added to the spreadsheet!"

I excitedly scooped them up and put them in my right back pocket. My usual storage spot is the left pocket, but clearly Ryan would be getting credit for these!

I chuckled because even though I had missed this enormous pile of pennies, they still ended up in my pocket. They still made it onto the spreadsheet. And they still became part of the bigger penny picture. I had chattered on about The Penny Project and picked up so many pennies myself, that Ryan couldn't possibly ignore the pile of pennies when he saw them. He knew how much this all meant to me.

By talking about what I wanted (pennies), I'd molded my world to give me just that. Not only am I tuned in to seeing pennies when I'm out and about, but I've created an army of penny finders who are equally skilled. All of this is because I can't help inviting people to play along with me.

I think in the long run, people want to help each other. It feels good to know you've made someone else's day. Whether you're sharing a found penny or helping a self-employed friend find work, there's something enjoyable about that human connection.

Come to think of it, it happens at my house every Christmas, too. Mom asks for a list of what I want. Most years I give it to her and get what's on it (with a few unexpected surprises thrown in). One year, I was too busy to make a list. Although the things she got me were lovely, they weren't what I would have asked for. And while she is smart and intuitive when it comes to me, she isn't a mind reader. No list meant that Mom didn't know what to give me! Whether it is making a list, updating your Facebook status or chatting over coffee, find a way to share your dreams.

Lesson

Don't be shy in telling people what your dreams are. Whether your dreams are about finding new clients, creating your Christmas wish list, or adding pennies to your spreadsheet (although I'd be surprised if THAT is on your dream list!), you're infinitely more likely to get support or information that will help you achieve those dreams by talking about them than if you never say anything at all.

And even if the people you know don't know exactly how to help, they probably know people who do. It's the six degrees of separation game.

Enthusiasm is contagious. So tap into those things that you want to talk about and you'll be surprised at how many people will listen. And your amazement will continue to grow when you discover the doors these people will open up for you. But you'll never know about those doors unless you give your dreams a voice.

What are your 2 cents?

- Who are your biggest supporters, the ones who really want you to succeed?
- What dreams do you have that could use a little boost?
- In what ways might you let your supporters know about your dreams?

The Other Side Of The Coin
Why When You Attract Your Opposite It's Not A Bad Thing & You Might Just Learn Something

Have you ever noticed that when you are really excited about something, other people want to tell you about all the other stuff you may not be considering? It's their yin to your yang. It's their peanut butter to your jelly. But sometimes, it just feels like the negative to your positive.

About a year and a half into my penny collecting, I went to an amazing conference. It was called CPSI (pronounced sip-see), which stands for the Creative Problem Solving Institute. My first facilitation mentor had told me about the conference.

When I was learning facilitation, he said facilitation is like dancing. There's a combination of art and structure. He said the classes I'd taken had given me great structure, like learning the technical steps of a tango. But he believed CPSI was where I could take my learning to the next level and start playing with the ART of facilitation. This would be the equivalent of picking the right music, costumes, choreography and "oomph" for a top-notch tango.

I wanted a rose in my teeth. I wanted to tango! So off I went to check out this CPSI thing of which he spoke so highly.

What a blast! He was totally right. My mind was stretched and, in addition to having some great structure, these folks were all creative. I was surrounded by professionals from many fields. The common thread was that they all wanted to bring creativity back to their lives and work.

As part of the class I'd registered for that week, I was lucky enough to be selected as a 'client' for one of the practice facilitation sessions we'd be doing. As the client, I asked for help coming up with ways to grow The Penny Project.

Our session turned out to be a blast! The leaders were creative and by the end of our time, we had four solid ideas to explore. The best part was the group actually got a lot of energy talking about the pennies! They loved the whole concept and were great participants in helping me come up with new ideas.

Of course, their energy fed my energy and I left class walking on air! I headed to lunch still chattering about pennies and possibilities.

Lunch was in a big room with open seating. I grabbed my food and joined a half full table. As we all started talking about what our mornings had been like, I couldn't help but share my excitement about The Penny Project.

I told the table about how we got started, some of the lessons I'd learned by saving pennies, and the great ideas my group had just come up with in our class. Everyone was excited for me. It was a great moment.

And then, out of nowhere, one of the guys at the table said, "I have a similar story. The only difference is…I hate pennies."

Wow. Talk about a buzz kill. Got any more rain you wanna throw on my parade, mister? And how in the name of all that's holy do you think hating pennies is remotely similar to ANYTHING I just said?

I was torn between telling this man to keep his nasty opinions to himself and asking what could possibly make someone hate a poor, unsuspecting penny.

But being a facilitator among facilitators at this conference, I thought it best to proceed with a question. "Why's that?" I asked, only half wanting to know this guy's answer, which I was sure would be totally lame.

"Well, I'll tell ya," he started out. "A few years ago I decided pennies just weren't worth the hassle."

I'd like to say I was keeping an open mind (and I probably looked like I was to the undiscerning observer, which would be just about everyone but my mother). But I was really wondering why this guy couldn't keep his penny-hate to himself instead of contradicting my love affair with them. I feigned interest as he continued.

"In fact, I grouped nickels and dimes in with them, too."

Had this man lost his mind? I go through the roof when I find something silver, and he's just ditching these coins as worthless?

"One day I did a rough calculation of how much it would cost me to leave small change behind — everything but quarters — whenever I bought something. I don't love having jingling change in my pocket and I also don't love figuring out what to do with it when it amasses at home."

"So what do you do when you get small change at a store?" I asked, now starting to get a little more curious.

"I leave it behind, everything but the quarters."

"Hmm," I said, as it began to occur to me that without guys like him, I might not find so much change in the checkout lanes at Target.

"You see, the calculation showed that over the course of a year, I'd leave behind less than $50 bucks if I did this. So I tried it out for awhile. I found I really liked it."

"And what was it you liked so much?" I countered, waiting for something in his story that sounded like it was tied to the points I had made earlier. So far, throwing away $50 a year in change wasn't helping me see what that might be.

"Well, leaving all that change behind taught me not to sweat the small stuff. I realized there were a whole lot more important things in my life than keeping track of loose change. Leaving the coins behind saves me time, or rather gives me time, to do the things I think are more important."

And there it was. I totally saw the connection.

Saving pennies taught me to pay attention to the little things in my life that are important. Leaving pennies behind taught this guy to ignore the little things in his life that AREN'T that important.

His story truly was the yin to my yang. Or more appropriately, the heads to my tails!

We ended up chatting for quite some time about our varying views on pennies. Both of us had learned valuable lessons from our experiments and were excited to share what we'd learned with others. We were kindred spirits brought together by pennies.

And although I'd initially been somewhat offended by this guy's disregard for pennies, in reality he was a dream come true for me — someone I could get behind at the grocery store and score a few pennies and dimes!

Lesson

Don't be so sure your opponents, enemies, or polar opposites don't have something to teach you. What may at first seem like an irreconcilable difference might turn out to be two sides of the same coin. In my case, that was quite literally true!

I once heard another facilitator say we all have the same values, but they just come in varying degrees. Does anyone believe we shouldn't educate our children? Or that we don't want to have a planet to live on in 10 years? We all basically want the same things, but we just see different ways to make those things happen.

So before you start World War III with someone who has an opposing view point (because it's so much easier to get defensive than it is to listen to their side of the story), ask a few questions. Do a little digging. And most importantly, be open to the fact you may not know it all.

What are your 2 cents?

- How do you let your parade get rained on?
- What do you do when other people don't share your values? Might they be the "heads to your tails?"
- What disagreements in your life could use a little more searching for common ground and a little less defensiveness?

Perspective

Why You May Get Way More Than Just What You See... If You Believe There's More To Get

Have you ever gotten involved in something that seemed so innocuous on the surface but ended up being way more than you bargained for?

That's exactly what happened when my sister got invited to a dinner where her mere attendance scored her a free iPod shuffle. AND, her invitation allowed for one additional guest, who would also receive an iPod. Guess who was first in line for that date?

What a deal! It sounded way too good to be true. Can you see where this might be going?

Clearly, this was a tactic to suck people in, and there were my sister and I at the head of the line. We showed up at the dinner, heard a sales pitch and then collected our door prize, which turned out to be the distant cousin of an iPod shuffle (or what my sister still refers to as the niPod buffle).

Worse yet, I had been convinced to buy a $50 software package to create my own website online. I'd wanted to create a website since

I'd established my company, so it wasn't TOTALLY ridiculous. But I felt a bit like I'd ignored all the good advice my dad gave me and all the good sense I thought I had.

The sales pitch continued as I was invited to a full day seminar to learn some of the ins and outs of the online tool I'd just purchased. This was clearly another sales pitch for an even BIGGER web design package.

Not thrilled that I felt sucked in yet again, I was initially closed off to everything they were telling me. I hemmed and hawed, sitting frustrated that I'd ended up in ANOTHER sales pitch. How dumb could I possibly be?!

In the middle of my pity party, a speaker got up to talk about some of the cool features this software could provide. Even skeptical, old me in the back of the room was engaged by this guy. In addition to telling us about the program, he was doling out advice about perspective.

He shared a story from a previous workshop where one of the participants had challenged him. The customer said he wanted time to go look for online reviews before committing to buy the product. The speaker asked the guy, "What kind of reviews are you going to look for?"

The guy didn't know exactly what to make of the question. "I'm going to look for reviews of the product," he said, as if it was the dumbest question he'd ever heard.

"I know that, but are you going to look for good reviews or bad reviews? If you answer that question right now, I know whether or not you're going to buy the product. Whatever kind of reviews you go out looking for, I guarantee you're going to find them."

"If you go out looking for good reviews," he continued "you've decided you like the product and want to back up that opinion. If you're searching for bad reviews, it's probably because you're skeptical and want to find confirmation that you're right. Either way, you're going to find what you're looking for."

I sat there for a moment sort of amazed by this guy's story. It made perfect sense. We go out every day in life and find the things we are looking for. If we look for good people, happy moments, and a generally positive experience, we find it. Conversely, if we go out looking for mean people, bad situations, and negativity, we find that, too.

As I sat in that room and was reminded about my choice of perspective, I couldn't help but think of the times I'd touted this same principle when it comes to pennies. My choice of perspective in regard to finding a penny is:

"It's just a penny."

or

"It's a PENNY!!!"

For me, the choice is easy. Every penny I find becomes more than just a penny — it's a bit of an experience, a moment to be thankful for the abundance in my life. Not only the abundance of pennies, but the abundance of supportive people, funny stories, shared connections, opportunities to give back, and unusual penny-related happenings.

Since starting this project, I have never picked up a coin and thought, "It's just a penny." Perhaps it's the perspective I've gained from tracking several years' worth of found money. Or it might be that this whole journey has taught me that there are no ordinary moments. Yes, even the seemingly mundane task of picking up a stray penny has become a joyous experience for me.

And the best part is…I'm not alone! Even today as I sat down to write this chapter, I got a call from my friend Nicole telling me she'd heard a coin drop behind her and actually turned around to see if she could find it. She waited to see if anyone was going to pick it up and when no one did, she scored a whole quarter!

We laughed and laughed. I told her she had become the equivalent of a Jedi-master in penny collecting. When one can HEAR the change drop and alters the route to go back and find it…THAT is true dedication!

I hope more than anything that these little moments my friends and family share with me via phone, e-mail, and text help them feel firsthand that, when it comes to pennies, you really do get way more than you see. A penny isn't just a penny when you pick it up and it makes you want to call a friend to share the story. That's when a penny becomes an experience!

Lesson

Everything, and I mean EVERYTHING, we do in life comes down to a choice of perspective. One of my favorite motivational speakers, Roger Crawford, once asked possibly the greatest question I've ever heard related to perspective:

"When you look outside, do you see bright sunshine or do you see a dirty window?"

More importantly, when you pass by a penny on the street do you play it cool and think "It's just a penny."? Or do you allow yourself to see a little bit more, to seize the moment, and to proclaim (even if only to yourself), "It's a PENNY!!!"?

What are your 2 cents?

- What do you see when you look out YOUR window?
- How's that perspective working out for you?
- What other perspectives might be possible if you choose to see them?

Worry

Why You're Probably Imagining It WAY Worse Than It Will Actually Turn Out

A s I sit down to write this chapter, I'm not even sure exactly what it's about. Typically, I come to the computer with an experience from my life, a story about pennies, and a theme connecting the two. This time, the connecting theme is eluding me.

So, I'm going to follow my own advice and take baby steps until a title for the chapter becomes obvious. What good is doling out brilliant advice if I never heed it myself? This is what one of my former army leaders called "eating your own dog food." If it's good enough for everyone else, then it should be good enough for me, too!

And now, with that, I'm ready to begin and see where this chapter takes me (and you!).

I've always fancied myself as quite responsible and reliable. I was a bit of a goodie-two-shoes growing up and never really seemed to mind being the good kid. Sure, I did some not-such-good-kid things every once in a while (Mom, Dad…sorry about chewing up the front end of the car trying to drive through the desert to get to a "cool kid" party that one time. Oh, and Grandma & Grandpa, thanks for remaining calm when I divulged the fact I have a tattoo at your 65th Anniversary celebration.)…but what kid didn't?

Even though I may have outgrown my goodie-two-shoes status (now I'm just called a nerd and viewed as eccentric and successful because of my "ways"), I'm still somewhat connected to the good kid image people had of me growing up. I make good decisions, I'm self-sufficient (except for the part about being on my family's cell phone plan, but who turns that down?!) and I'm trustworthy.

So when I was visiting home a few weeks ago and my mom gave me the locket HER mom gave to her to wear at her wedding (I was supposed to pass it on to my sister to wear at her upcoming wedding), I was 100% certain I was up for the task of taking it where it needed to go.

The time between that visit and my parents coming over for the holidays was short. In the rush of unpacking, cleaning, and trying to wrap up end of the year financial data for my company, I forgot to pass the locket on to my sister. I hadn't even remembered it until she brought it up at her house during Christmas.

"No problem," I thought. I know where that is. "I'll get it out and set it aside so you can grab it the next time you're at my house."

But then I went home and promptly realized I had no clue where the locket was. I checked the place I thought I'd left it…no locket. So I pulled out the bag I'd taken on the trip and thought maybe I'd left it in one of those pockets. Nope, not there either.

I was on a bit of a tight schedule as I had a plane to catch in just a few hours. I decided to spend 20 more minutes doing my best to find the thing. I tore my jewelry organizer, purse, and even my kitchen apart (I'd last seen it in a plastic bag and thought it might have been put with others of its kind).

No luck.

I felt awful. Not only had I lost an heirloom that meant a lot to my mom, but I'd also sort of destroyed my sister's "something old" item for her wedding. Not good.

I knew I had to get ready for my trip and couldn't dedicate anymore time to my search. I also knew I didn't want to spend the next 10 days worrying about having to tell my mom & sister the locket was gone. So I called my mom to tell her the bad news.

Now, my family is pretty good about stuff like this. A dish breaks or a camera gets stolen on vacation and they spend about a minute or so feeling miffed about what just happened. Then, they say, "Well, is the story of this vacation going to be a stolen camera or a good time?" They always opt for the good time.

I knew ultimately my mom wasn't going to disown me for losing the necklace, but I was ready for a few minutes of chastising and sniveling about having lost a treasured family heirloom. I was also ready for the certainty that my sister would now demand SHE be known as the responsible sister.

I wasn't looking forward to either conversation.

I started by calling my mom since it was her locket I'd lost.

Turns out my worry and dread weren't necessary at all. My mom's take on it was, "Oh, that's a bummer. But it's just a thing. And if we're meant to have it for the wedding, it will turn up." Then she told me her mom had lost a watch once and didn't find it until 10 years later when they were moving out of their house. She told me she wasn't going to be surprised if that's what happened with the locket!

By the time I got off the phone with my mom, I didn't have time to call my sister because I needed to finish packing and get to the airport. When I finally arrived at my flight gate, my sister had already talked to my mom and sent me a text message about it. This is typical for my family, by the way. My sister's comment wasn't as bad as I thought it would be. In fact, it was pretty nice considering I was a total buffoon for losing this thing:

Do u really think the locket is gone? Is there any hope it's only misplaced? I'm holding out hope that you'll find it. Positive thoughts. Positive thoughts.

I felt a little better, but still wanted to talk to her and tell her I was sorry. The plane was boarding, so now wasn't the time. I turned my phone off and boarded my flight.

It's an amazing thing, the mind. When you let go of what's worrying you, it seems the answer pops right up as if it was just waiting for you to stop resisting the fact that, deep down, you already know the answer to the question you're asking. Sometime mid-flight, I realized I hadn't checked my backpack! THAT is where I'd put the baggie with the locket in it!

As soon as I landed, I sent my sister a text letting her know she was right — there was hope!

Me: I really thought I lost the locket…that's why I called Mom. But I thought of one more place to look today! I'll check it when I get back. Positive thoughts. Positive thoughts!

Sis: Ok. I'm not too worried about it. I know we'll find it!

Wow. The responses I'd gotten all throughout this journey were so different than I had imagined they would be. And it wasn't like I was expecting the worst — I knew my family was pretty good when it came to stuff like this (my poor Mom has had practice dealing with her list of items lost, stolen and broken, including her wedding ring and a piece of furniture her dad made her. It's all like water off a duck's back now!).

But even knowing my family was good with this stuff, I had created a worst case scenario in my head.

It reminded me of the time my penny tracking sheet crashed. The thumb drive where I kept the data got corrupted and my file turned to strings of random letters and numbers. Not good.

I had sent an update about a month prior, so at least I had that data. But all the found and donated money between July 29 and September 3 were toast. I could figure the grand total based on what was in the account, but I was not going to be able to attribute it to the right people.

I felt really bad about this. All of the people in the project were so supportive and really kind to play along with my crazy ideas that I honestly dreaded telling them that some of the change they'd donated was lost. Well, not ACTUALLY lost, but their credit for it might be lost.

I typed out an update with the highlights of the last few months. Big finds, donated money, and the fact we'd made our first charitable donation of $500 to a conference geared at helping young women build self-esteem .

Then I told them the bad news. The penny file had been corrupted and although the total was not affected, individual contributors might not get full credit for the money they'd given me.

I hit send and waited for the annoyed e-mails to roll in.

After a week, you know how many angry, annoyed e-mails I'd received? None! Not a single angry message saying, "Man, that sucks…I donated a lot of change in August. Why don't you back up your data better?"

I did, however, get several e-mails from people saying they felt bad for me as they knew how much The Penny Project meant to me. Others skipped over the bad news completely and just congratulated me on the $500 donation to charity.

Again, this was not what I had been expecting. Although when I thought about it, I had to laugh at myself. I wasn't dealing with multi-million dollar investments here. These were people who were giving me found money, the sums of which rarely totaled anything over $1. At that rate, it's not worth getting mad about, is it? Besides, people who willingly give up money for a good cause probably aren't going to be angry they don't get credit for their 47¢ as long as it still goes to the cause.

Although I realized all of this after the fact, it hadn't stopped me from assuming the worst and being ready for angry tirades from the people on my sheet, tirades that never came. And worry, therefore, that was wasted.

Lesson

And so, after writing these stories, here is the theme I've discovered: don't waste undue time worrying about things that may or may not happen, or things that have already happened. The emotional knot you put in your stomach is likely unwarranted. And even if things do seemingly take a turn for the worse, dreading it is probably not the best use of your time. What does all of that worry and trepidation get you in the end, anyway?

Consider this: if things don't turn out as you had planned, you have to deal with them regardless of how much time you spent worrying. So, if your time dealing with the awful outcome is X, why tack on the Y of worrying? X+Y= too much time! Just skip the worry phase and deal with X when and IF — and that's a big if — it happens.

Most of the time, we worry about things that never come to fruition. On top of that, when we worry, we end up focusing on the very things we don't want to happen, which makes them infinitely more likely to happen because we are LOOKING for them!

That's why, despite my minimal worry, I called my mom immediately when I thought I lost the locket. It's also why I sent a timely update telling people what went wrong with the penny data. Bad news doesn't get better with time and waiting to share it only increases your worry factor.

Oh, are you worried about the necklace? You shouldn't be, I found it!

What are your 2 cents?

- What things do you worry about in your daily life?
- Think of a time when your worry was completely wasted. How would you do it differently now?
- What can you do the next time you feel worry creeping in to stop it and just deal with the problem head on?

Goals

Why It's Perfectly Okay NOT To Always Have A Goal

I have to admit something. When I first started picking up pennies, I didn't have a goal in my head about where it would lead, or even how many I'd pick up. In fact, I wasn't sure I'd find many pennies at all. I figured I couldn't be the only one keeping an eye out for money in the streets. Surely there were enough other people out there who picked up coins that I'd only find the occasional penny every now and then.

Boy, how wrong was I?!

The other day, I heard a story about a goal setting lecture given to a friend's daughter while she was at a Girl Scout meeting.

As a facilitator, I love clever exercises that prove points to groups I'm working with. Whether they instill learning about teamwork, communication styles or any other number of topics, most people remember far more by doing than they will by hearing a simple lecture.

That's why I loved this story about the Girl Scout meeting so much. Instead of just telling the girls about how to set good goals for themselves, the speaker did an exercise to help the girls experience this concept first hand.

He asked the girls to snap their fingers as many times as they could in a minute.

Go ahead, set the book down and try it if you want to! I didn't have a stop watch with me when I heard the story, but I did try to snap as fast as I could for a few seconds. I wanted to have an idea just how fast I snapped.

When the guy said stop, he asked the girls how many times they'd snapped during that minute. They shouted out their answers. I imagine some girls looking rather pleased with themselves for doing better than the others, as if there was going to be a badge awarded for best snapper!

Part two of the exercise required a bit of math. The speaker asked the girls to figure out how many times they would have to snap if they improved their original number by 10%. Once they had that figured out, he gave them another minute and asked them to repeat the exercise, only this time with that goal number in mind.

When they were done, every girl had achieved her goal. His lecture went on to explain that what they'd experienced is the basic concept of goal setting. When a task is new, you might not know how many, how much, or how long your initial goal should be, so you just do it for a while to determine your base.

As you gather data (in this case, snapping for a minute), you can begin to stretch yourself by setting goals higher than what you were able to achieve by just doing the task without a goal.

I thought it was a great exercise to introduce kids to goal setting. I also thought it sounded exactly like how I set goals when I started The Penny Project.

When I first embarked on my penny finding journey, I had absolutely NO idea what was a reasonable number of pennies to expect to find in a year. Would I find a few per day? Or maybe it would be more like a few per week?

Since goals are meant to propel us forward, not hold us back, I had decided to just jump in and see how much money I could find.

This is why I tracked it all on a spreadsheet. To me, data is fun! It can tell us things we might not have otherwise known. What months are better for penny finding? What coin is found the most often? How much does the average person find in a year?

After about six months, I averaged out my daily balance of penny finding. At that time, I was averaging about 9 cents per day. I thought this was quite fantastic and wanted to keep that average up through the rest of the year. I ended the year with $32.76, which averaged out to fewer than 9 cents per day. I thought this was pretty good for a first attempt.

For the second year, I decided to set my sights a little higher. I was going to aim for an average of 11 cents per day. This would get me to about $40 for the year, which I thought was a great goal for a penny finder!

Throughout the year, I kept an eye on my average. It was pretty close to 11 cents per day and I was on target to hit my $40 goal for the year.

And then, a few weeks before the end of the year, I found a $10 bill. I was SO excited! This helped boost my total tremendously and put me at $55.42 for the year — a 15 cent per day average. This was way better than I had hoped. I was glad my goal pushed me to keep up the penny finding!

As I entered my third year of penny finding, I wasn't sure what to do. I knew the $10 bill was a great stroke of luck and had helped boost me to a 15 cent per day total. Should I set that as my new goal or bring it back down to a more realistic 12 cent per day goal (my average without the $10 bill)?

I decided to keep my goal at 15 cents. I knew it was going to be a stretch, but thought it was better to set a difficult (yet achievable) goal and miss it than to set an easy goal and achieve it.

I didn't find any big paper money in year three (except for a $1 bill in Disneyland — it really IS the happiest place on earth!) but I still managed to find $55.06, which still averages out to over 15 cents per day!

Although my total was lower, I had actually found more CHANGE than I had the previous year. Not to mention a few other things I'd accomplished:

- I'd figured out new places to find money (toll booths — big scores at toll booths in year two!)
- I grew the penny finder base, which had improved our overall total collected by 27%
- I donated our first money to charity
- I started writing about the lessons I'd learned from pennies

When I looked at it that way, I felt like I'd actually improved from year two to year three, even if my individual total for the year was slightly lower.

And to me, that's what goal setting is all about.

Goals are meant to help us improve, to spur growth, and to make sure we continue striving for our full potential. They are NOT meant to keep us from trying things because we don't want to fail or to make us feel bad when we don't achieve them.

Lesson

Have fun with your goals. Set them in a way that is motivating to you and makes you want to get out there and achieve them.

And don't worry if you don't have any goals at first! Do what you love for a while and then determine how you can get incrementally better. Rome wasn't built in a day. I didn't collect hundreds of dollars in found money overnight. And whatever your goals are, they're meant to help you get where you're going over time, not instantaneously!

What are your 2 cents?

- What areas of your life could use a little goal setting?
- What data can you collect to help you determine a goal that is achievable, but will stretch you to do your best?
- And to keep it fun, how will you reward yourself when the mission is accomplished?

How Bad You Want It
Why When You Really Want Something Bad Enough You Don't Care What Other People Think

Depending on how you look at it, my most (or least) shining moment in penny finding came when I discovered a grate outside my accountant's office.

It was mid-winter 2009 and I had to trudge down to my accountant's office for my tax reconciliation of the previous year. It was cold in DC at the time and I wasn't totally thrilled to be out and about in the sub-freezing weather.

But it was easier for me to walk to the appointment than to drive or take the bus, so I gladly took that option and got a little exercise (and penny finding opportunities along the way, of course) on my way to see how much I owed in taxes.

Just outside my accountant's office, I passed a grate that sat under a parking meter. Since I always pay attention around parking meters, I just happened to look down through the grate.

Under the metal cover sat several pennies, nickels, dimes, and QUARTERS! I couldn't believe the bounty I saw just a few inches under the surface. I was ecstatic…and then a little depressed.

Unfortunately, I didn't have time before the appointment to figure out a way to recover the change under the grate. Not that I didn't try for a minute or two, mind you. But eventually, not wanting to be late, I gave up the fight, headed up to my appointment, and tried to focus on the task at hand.

I spent the next hour working with my accountant trying to figure out the best way for me to maximize my tax return. It was a productive hour, but when it was over, I was excited to return to my change-filled grate outside.

Yes, my brilliant accountant had just saved me thousands in taxes and all I could think about was the loose change outside her office. Nice.

On the way down the elevator, I remembered that there was a food court in the basement of the building and, better yet, it had a Japanese place. I got pretty excited when I realized I could probably secure chopsticks from them to do some ingenious McGyver-type work on that grate to recover the change just beneath it!

Flash forward a few minutes later and there I was, on my knees with chopsticks in hand, going after the coins under the grate. I tried for the quarters first as they were the biggest finds. I easily recovered them and moved on to the dimes and nickels. It wasn't exactly easy to pick up change with chopsticks, but I was so excited by the idea of recovering over a dollar in change, that I didn't care how challenging it was!

The longer I stayed crouched over the grate, the more people walked by looking at me in dismay. I caught plenty of perplexed stares, shaking heads, and whispers as I fished for the change. I was dressed in gym wear, which didn't exactly help me blend in downtown. And of course, I was fishing for quarters with chopsticks. These people probably thought I was homeless!

At first, the shaking heads and sad looks got to me. Then I remembered, "These folks have no idea who I am, what I'm doing, or why I'm doing it — what do I care if they give me odd stares?!"

So I continued to chopstick the coins to the tune of $1.82. I was pretty pleased with myself for the change I'd recovered. And rightfully so! It wasn't easy picking pennies out of a grate with chopsticks!

The first person I called was my neighbor, Marissa. She wasn't exactly a fan of The Penny Project. More like a regular mocker who laughed at my silliness in penny finding. She answered the phone and laughed hysterically as I shared with her my latest penny-finding caper. Yes, she thought I was ridiculous. But, she also got a fantastic chuckle from my story, and what's better than making a friend laugh?!

Next, I called my dad. He also got a good laugh and said, "Good for you!" It's always nice to have one person in your corner when you're doing something a little crazy, I think.

After we hung up, I decided to visit my friend Illeny at her office since I was close by and knew she would enjoy my story as she had a similar penchant to mine for penny finding. When I got to her desk and poured the change out of my pocket, she was predictably excited, laughed one of those fun, contagious laughs, and congratulated me on my huge find!

It occurred to me at that moment that the entire time I'd been picking up loose change from the grate with those chopsticks, I was actually having a great time. And not only was I having a great time THEN, but I was having a great time NOW sharing my story with friends and family. After all, the end result was that my seemingly crazy antics landed me almost $2! Who cares what those people who walked by me thought? I had a goal to achieve, and it wasn't to impress them. It was to add to The Penny Project's bottom line.

Then I began to relate this on a bigger scale. When do people create goals they care more about than impressing others? And, along those lines, what goals do businesses have that they care more about than making a single customer, or employee, happy? Are there any? If so, what are they?

We are so likely to get caught up in what other people think that we often abandon our own dreams and goals. Or, maybe the things we are doing don't invoke that "I don't care what others think" kind of passion, which is why we so easily leave them behind when they don't fit in with what others think we should be doing.

Lesson

Take some time to think about the things you want in life. I mean the things you REALLY want. The ones that even if the love of your life looked at you like you were a lunatic, you still wouldn't abandon them.

These are the things that ignite passion inside of us. We want them so badly that we don't stop to worry about what other people think.

In the end, ironically, it is this kind of passion that is attractive to people. So even if the task isn't to their liking, the passion and excitement you exude — because it is to YOUR liking — will be intoxicating to them.

If I can tell a tale of fishing pennies out of a grate with chopsticks and have people ooh-ing and aah-ing over my story, surely the things that ignite your passion are worth pursuing!

What are your 2 cents?

- What are the things that ignite a spark within you?
- What things do you enjoy doing so much that you'd do them even if no one did them with you?
- How can you bring more of that into your life, regardless of what anyone thinks?

Timing
Why "I Want It NOW" Didn't Work For Veruca Salt & It Won't Work For You

Have you ever seen the movie Willie Wonka & the Chocolate Factory? If you haven't, I'm going to have to insist you put this book down right now and go watch it. Seriously! Book down! You're missing out. It's a classic.

But make sure to get the older version with Gene Wilder. I'm sure Johnny Depp is great in the remake (and fun to look at for a few hours), but you just can't beat Gene Wilder's response when Veruca asks, "Schnozberries? Who's ever heard of a schnozberry?"

We are the music makers...and *we* are the dreamers of dreams.

Great stuff! But I digress.

What was I talking about? Oh yes…timing. Willy Wonka. Right.

There's a whole song in Willy Wonka called "I Want It Now" in which a bossy little daddy's girl named Veruca Salt simply can't stand not having her way at the very moment she wants it, which leads to her untimely departure, down a garbage shoot.

I have to laugh at that scene in the movie because I see people doing it so often. They demand, coerce, and insist, "Give it to me NOW!" when in fact, later would be just fine.

We have become a bit of an instantaneous society. With the advent of microwaves and cell phones, if we can't eat 60 seconds after deciding we're hungry, or immediately get a hold of someone on the phone, we think something's wrong.

But maybe, just maybe, there's a reason we're not getting what we want right now. Is it possible there's something better down the line?

I learned this lesson when Illeny found a $20 bill on the ground during the third year of the Penny Project. By then, she had logged well over $100 in found money and we'd shared numerous texts, calls, stories, and laughs.

Although we rarely texted about anything smaller than a quarter, she actually CALLED me the day she found a $20 bill in the Whole Foods parking lot. That was exciting! In fact, I think it was the first $20 bill we'd found since the original $20 bill that started the whole project.

When she told me about it, I was really excited. Twenty bucks was a big find! And since I'd just made my first donation to charity, the penny coffers were a lot lower than normal. I couldn't wait to collect the $20 bill from her. Score!!

Only, there was a problem. Illeny was unemployed at the time and not sure she wanted to give the $20 bill up, at least, not right away. She wanted to carry it around in her purse for a while to feel the abundance of that HUGE find.

Although this was understandable, I was a bit flustered. I couldn't really argue. She was the one who'd found the money. And it was, after all, hers to do with as she pleased.

But if she called me to crow about it, I thought the least she could do was donate it to the cause. Surely she wouldn't miss money that wasn't hers at the start of the day.

Although I really, REALLY wanted to say, "Alright you nincompoop… give me the $20!" I decided against it. I thought if I did that, I was actually going to be the nincompoop in that conversation.

So, I settled on adding it to the "Accounts Receivable" column of the spreadsheet and forgetting about it for the time being.

A few months later, I got a text message from Illeny. She had just found ANOTHER $20 bill.

What the hell?! Was there some crazy admirer walking around in front of her dropping paper money for her to find? She'd also found a $10, a $5, and four $1's that year. She was on a roll!

Although I deal with pennies every day and talk to Illeny several times a week, I'd all but forgotten about her previous $20 until she found the second one. And it turned out that was just what she needed to help her let go of the first one.

She came to my house later that week to deliver the first $20 and some other change she'd found. She was still in job search mode, but promised when she got a job, she'd give me the second one, too.

Wow! That was a big score! A big score that probably wouldn't have happened if I'd gone all Veruca Salt on her and demanded she give me the first $20 bill NOW!

Much of life, it turns out, is all about timing. More specifically, it's about honoring the timing of others.

In the long run, did it REALLY matter if I got that $20 bill from Illeny the day she found it or two months later? Was my need to have it now more important than her need to feel the abundance of a found $20 bill in her purse while she was in job search mode in a down economy?

The answer to both questions is NO!

And boy am I glad I figured that out. Not only did Illeny give me that first $20 bill she found, but a month later she got a job and gave me the SECOND $20 bill she found, effectively catapulting her to the top money-finder of 2009 (a coveted title that only I had held until that point).

If I had demanded HER big find on MY timeline, I'd probably have ended up with neither $20 bill going to the bottom line of the penny fund. Good thing I stopped myself from becoming a "bad egg" (another movie reference — go see it if you don't know what that means!).

Lesson

A really smart colleague of mine once told a roomful of our facilitation students, "Facilitation takes as long as it takes."

You know what? So does life!!! It's easy to forget this when we spend one too many days with our micro-waved breakfasts in one hand and cell phone pressed against our ears with the other.

I found out from Illeny that PEOPLE also take as long as they're going to take. Just because their timelines don't match our own, doesn't mean we have the right to rush them, or that we need to let them rush US for that matter!

What are your 2 cents?

In the midst of your next go-go-go day (because you know we all have them), remember to take a deep breath and ask yourself:

- What things do I need to give a little more time to?
- Whose timing can I do a better job of honoring?
- How can I ask other people to better honor my timing?
- What things might I be losing out on by pushing too hard and ignoring the importance of timing?

Perfection

Why You Might Want To Reconsider The Phrase "Practice Makes Perfect"

If I've said it once, I've said it a million times. Perfect circles don't occur in nature.

And every time I DO say it, my sister tells me I sound like Rain Man.

But it IS true, you know. Perfect circles DON'T occur in nature. That's why I'm able to find so many pennies. When I see a perfect circle out of the corner of my eye, I can be certain it will be a penny (or possibly some other manmade object like a bottle cap).

And when you think about it, isn't "perfection" sort of a manmade object in and of itself? Sure, we can AIM for perfection, but can we really achieve it?

In the facilitation course I teach, there's a slide in the intro that says:

"Practice Makes _____"

I always put it up and ask the class what they think. Inevitably, some Type-A perfectionist screams out, "PERFECT!" (I know about these people because I'm a recovering Type-A perfectionist myself!).

It's about that time that they realize this class is going to be a little different. This class isn't going to be about getting 100% on some test at the end. It's going to be about digging in, trying new techniques, and sometimes, making a mess of things.

They discover this because this slide prompts a discussion about what practice REALLY makes. We offer the following ideas:

- Practice Makes Permanent (if you practice wrong, you do it wrong)
- Practice Makes Progress (practice helps you get continually better)

The class is set up as a 4-day course in which students get six chances to do hands-on exercises practicing what they've learned. The goal is to acquire permanent skills that they can use to move forward by the end of the sixth practice session.

I throw students into the deep end since I only give them 10 minutes of prep time to facilitate a mini-session in front of their peers.

Or at least it felt like the deep end to me when I took the class!

But as an instructor, I like the manufactured rush. Mostly because life's full of manufactured rushes we don't get to control. Deadlines, extra requirements for the boss, you name it!

Practicing under rushed conditions when you barely feel like you know what you're doing, gives you the confidence to do it under regular conditions knowing you've lived through worse.

But the real value of the class comes in letting people know it is okay to fail.

I actually learned this lesson in a series of coaching classes I took. In our first class, the facilitators asked us to really stretch and try things we weren't comfortable with. Things we thought we might not be able to handle. Things we were pretty sure we'd fail at (like not ending a sentence in a preposition, for example, which I clearly just failed at, twice.)

They went beyond talking about failure being okay by actually CELEBRATING it. They even had nametags that said "Celebrate Failure" with little balloons and confetti all over them.

When they handed me one of those "Yay! I failed" nametags, I have to admit, I wasn't all that comfortable. Didn't people hire coaches because they DIDN'T want to fail? I got the concept of trying new things, but wasn't this taking it a bit too far?

I played along and went ever so slightly beyond my comfort zone. On a scale of 1 to 10, I'd say I gave it a "2" on the trying to fail spectrum — more than nothing, but not by much.

Thank goodness there were five classes in the series! With each one I got a little braver. By the end of the course, I was totally willing to try things that were sure to fail. Sometimes they surprised me and worked!! Other times I was just honest with my client (a fellow student) and said, "I don't think this is working, do you mind if we try something else?" And we did.

It was as simple as that. Fail, acknowledge it, and move on. In doing that, I was ready for the next opportunity to help my client make a big discovery. Failing didn't mean I was a failure, it only meant I was trying something new.

If we never try anything new or different, where does that leave us? Sure, we may not mess anything up. We may get a 100% on the test because we knew all the answers. But have we actually learned anything? Have we grown?

Failing is part of the cycle of life. That's what leads us to the next thing that DOES work. Post-its were created because some scientist failed to make glue that was sticky enough. The substance didn't work as glue, but it sure as heck worked to transform the way Americans leave notes.

Was it a failure because the glue the scientist was TRYING to make didn't work? Or was it a success because the by-product became an everyday staple in offices and homes across the country?

If the scientist had been "perfect" and achieved his mission, would there ever have been post-it notes?

Even my "perfect" theory that perfect circles don't occur in nature leads me astray at times. I've been known to pick up the occasional wooden nickel, construction site slug, bottle cap, and yes, even old, dried up chewing-gum has fooled me once or twice (this is why I always carry hand sanitizer in my purse!).

But sometimes my mistakes lead me to actual pennies that were lying just beyond their circular friends. Failing isn't the end of the line, it's a pit stop. And quite often, success is just ahead. Like that scientist with the "failed" glue, going for those "perfect circles" usually leads me to something good!

Lesson

Leave perfection for Hollywood movies and airbrushed models. And for God's sake, don't let the idea that you need to be perfect stop you from trying new things because you might fail.

Embrace failure. Seek opportunities to fail (even if it's just a little). Reframe your idea of failure as a final resting place — it's only one stop on your journey.

Just remember, if you're not failing, you're not trying. So the next time you think you see a "perfect circle in nature," grab it without a thought. And if it turns out to be an old piece of chewing gum, pull the hand sanitizer out of your bag, wipe your hands off, and keep your eyes peeled for the opportunity that failure may have just opened up to you.

What are your 2 cents?

- Where does a fear of failure keep you from growing?
- How can you dabble in failure to see what you learn?
- When might failure actually help you?

Community
Why People Tweeting In Cyberspace Might Be On To Something

When I first heard about Twitter, I thought the web had gone just a little too far. We already had MySpace and Facebook to share our EVERY move with people. Did we really need a site that was made up solely of headlines?

What could anyone have to say in 140 characters that would possibly be of any interest?

- I'm having turkey for lunch. TWEET!
- The skies are gray and I am blue. TWEET!
- Off to the bathroom… TWEET!

The thought of it was too much to bear.

But everywhere I turned there were people talking about it. Morning shows, commercials, even news sources got involved. I guess what finally made me cave was the competition between CNN and Ashton Kutcher to be the first tweeter to get to 1,000,000 followers.

I created an account and followed Ashton. What can I say? I'm more amused by Punk'd than I am informed by Larry King Live.

At first, I didn't really pay too much attention to the site. Sure, I had an account. I even logged on and tweeted the occasional message. I'm sure all three of my followers were thrilled.

But one day, I logged on and started digging around to see what kind of people were out there. Not that there's a ton of information on a user's page. Your "bio" is restricted to about 160 characters plus the link to a website or blog.

But I began searching to see what I could find.

The thing that really surprised me was how much great information people were sharing.

I searched by topics that were of interest to me at the time: coaching, law of attraction, leadership, and women's issues. Each search turned up lists of tweets on those topics. From there I could click on the individuals who'd made those tweets and see what else they were saying.

In a matter of hours, I'd found hundreds of interesting people, had some quick, witty conversations, and had discovered tons of useful articles, websites, and blogs. It was quite the opposite of what I'd thought Twitter was all about.

As I continued to find gobs of useful information and make connections on Twitter, I noticed several people commented on the great sense of community the site provided.

Huh! Community in 140 characters or less?

When I stepped back and looked at it, I realized they were right. Twitter, like any other social networking tool, can be used in a number of ways. Are there people out there who abuse it and send out spam-like tweets? Absolutely!

But if you get past that and find the people who want to provide interesting information and support other like minded individuals, it's a really amazing site!

And what's more, it's the site that led to me meeting my friend Tia, who let me do a guest blog post on her site, which was the seed that sprouted into this book!

When I thought of it that way, I had to laugh that I'd been such a critic before.

How is it that a girl who picks up pennies out of the gutter and tries to convince people that there is great joy in the little things in life couldn't see that there might be value in 140 characters or less?

I started thinking of each tweet as a penny. Each one has value and the sum total of Twitter is a community of people that get joy out of sharing what they know and learn from others. And isn't that the kind of community many of us seek, or the kind of success we all envision for our projects?

Community exists in lots of different aspects of our lives — work, church, clubs, activities, and yes, even online. Community doesn't have to remain confined to the ways we've traditionally viewed it in the past. And the more into the computer age we get, the more ways we'll have to create communities!

Plenty of great communities exist out there in cyberspace, just waiting to be discovered. From church choirs to websites with live meet-ups for activities such as bowling and board games, whether you want spiritual growth or just plain fun (or maybe a combination of both), there are tons of great groups tailor-made for your brand of community.

And if all else fails, create your own community! You could, for instance, begin picking up all the money you find and then see if others will join you in an effort to raise money for…

Wait. That one's taken. But feel free to create your own chapter!

Lesson

It's easy to discount something you don't understand. To look at a group of people and wonder, "What DO they see in that thing they are all focused on??"

But perhaps what they see doesn't lie in the WAY they've connected, but in the connections themselves.

Anything that brings people together is a way to build community. Whether it's a pair of friends playing a game over coffee or an online population of millions swapping information in 140-character banter, a sense of connection exists when people share an experience.

That's why I've loved the pennies so much. Sure, it was fun to track my finds those first few months of searching (by now, you know that I do love a good spreadsheet!). But the first time another person showed interest and shared their found money, The Penny Project became a community. (Thanks, Illeny, for being my first community builder!)

Communities bring value to our lives. And THAT's how the 140-character messages in Twitter appear to me now — as a valued way to connect with like-minded people. Each one a penny in my virtual bank!

What are your 2 cents?

- What communities are you a part of?
- What interests might draw you to new communities?
- What value do you find in being part of a community?
- What, if anything, has turned you away from the idea of community? How might you overcome your fears of "connecting?"

Making A Mountain Out of A Molehill

Why Sometimes Making A Big Deal About A Small Thing Is Just What The Doctor Ordered

Generally, I find it's not a best practice to blow things out of proportion. Some things are mountains. Others are molehills. There are certainly exceptions, but usually there's no need to make a mountain out of a molehill.

To me, a penny is the epitome of a molehill. It's small, inconspicuous, and generally not a big deal.

That's not to say I haven't made them into mountains at times.

Sometimes I crack myself up by embarrassing my friends who are too cool for picking up pennies by making a big deal of finding one in a checkout line or at a metro stop.

I tell the whole penny story to people standing nearby, get out the business cards, invite them to check out the blog, and go on and on about how cool spreadsheets are. It's a good time! In that case, the big deal (or mountain) carries me away to my happy place, which is atop that mountain having a good laugh about making my friends blush over a penny.

Juvenile, I know. But so much fun!

Well, it turns out I'm not the only one who can use pennies to get to a happier place.

One of the most touching notes I've received during the course of The Penny Project was from my friend Rachel. She married a good friend of mine from college and I got the chance to meet her at our 10-year class reunion. She's one of those people you like immediately and fits right in with the group. It felt like I'd known her for ages!

So, of course, I shared the story of The Penny Project with her and what I was doing with the money. She thought it was great and asked to be included in the updates.

Always happy to have another penny finder out there (having her was going to expand the operation into Wisconsin…woo hoo!), I happily added her to the update list.

Rachel and I kept in touch over the following months. I sent her the penny updates and even got the occasional e-mail telling me she'd found a penny or dime. The first few finds are always fun. The increased awareness and being on the lookout for a "big find" makes pennies exciting again!

Then one day, I got the following message. It was the end of a pretty standard week for me, but had obviously been a bit tougher for Rachel. Their daughter had been struggling with some undiagnosed health issues, which must be hard for a parent to deal with. In the midst of all she had going on, I was truly moved she found the time to write me this note.

Leslie~

Thanks for the penny update. Things here have been a little rough. We finally got a diagnosis for our little girl. She has Glucose Transporter Type 1 Deficiency Syndrome (GLUT1 DS). It's super rare (only about 200 cases diagnosed world-wide), but thankfully she has the type that is less severe and there is a treatment. It involves a low carb/ protein HIGH fat diet (ketogenic diet). Anyway, to my point (finally), we had her in the hospital trying to start the diet but failed (which was a huge bummer, but we'll try again soon... she's a stubborn 2 y/o with a bit of an eating disorder). BUT...I found 11¢! It made my otherwise horrible week a little bit happy. I love your penny project because it really does help me focus on the little joys in life.

So my total is now 22¢. 2 dimes and 2 pennies. I'm on the lookout all the time, but obviously people in Milwaukee keep better track of their money than people in the DC area so I haven't been finding much. Let me know how I send it in or what to do with it. It's in a little cup by my monitor so I don't have it with the rest of my change (it's special) :).

In that moment, I was so grateful I'd started The Penny Project. If it never accomplished anything but easing the worry of a sick child's mother, it had been worth it!

But beyond being glad about what I'd started, I was even MORE grateful that I had shared it with Rachel.

She had turned 11 found cents into a little bit of joy. In fact, it was enough joy to make her horrible week a little bit happy. And that's EXACTLY what I mean about the times it's perfectly ok to make a mountain out of a molehill!

I realized by reading her note that when something makes us feel better, brings us joy, or makes us happy, we should hold on to it for as long as possible. Talk about it, smile about it, and/or share e-mails about it — ride that good-vibe feeling for as long as we can!

And hopefully, before that good feeling ends, we'll find another penny (literal or figurative) to start the whole process over again.

I still love getting texts, phone calls, or e-mail messages about found money. Each one lets me know someone out there is doing a little "mountain building." But Rachel's message will always hold a special place in my heart for teaching me that even in the most challenging of times, there is ALWAYS a way to find joy and share it with others.

Lesson

It's really easy to make mountains out of molehills in the traditional sense — to hang on to hurt feelings or continually bring up a past mistake. But how does that really serve us in the end?

Wouldn't it be better to make our mountains out of the joyful molehills in our lives? The chats with friends we haven't connected with in awhile. The compliments one gets about a killer outfit. The little joys — yes, like finding pennies — that happen every day, but we often overlook?

The next time you're in the middle of a really bad week, think back to Rachel's message. Then find yourself a good molehill, climb on top of it, and stay there until you've created a mountain of happy thoughts.

It's your choice. Do you want to put yourself on a mountain of good or a molehill of evil?

What are your 2 cents?

- What kind of molehills do you choose to make into mountains?
- How do these mountains benefit you?
- What small joys can you make into your NEW molehills when things aren't going so well?

Taking The Road Less Traveled

Why With The Right Attitude, All Roads Lead To Joy

"The Road Not Taken" by Robert Frost is one of my favorite poems. Always having been one for doing what everyone else was not (gee, you don't say, Ms. Pick-up-pennies-from-the-gutter), I find it speaks to me. Especially the last few lines:

Two roads diverged in a wood, and I,

I took the one less traveled by,

And that has made all the difference.

The other day I had to walk downtown. Before I left the house, I thought about the route I would take to get to my destination. I tend to do this when I have to go anywhere because I want to walk where I'll have the highest probability of finding pennies. This usually means walking on major streets, preferably with parking meters and stores. Commerce draws people. People have money, money that they drop when they're trying to load up the parking meters.

It all makes perfect sense. And cents!

Keeping that in mind, I decided to take 14th Street all the way down to M Street, which is where my appointment was. 14th Street is a major thoroughfare with shops, banks, and restaurants along a parking meter lined street. In other words, 14th Street is my gold mine.

I set out for what was going to be about a 35 minute walk on a frigid winter day.

I'd walked about four blocks on 14th Street when I hit what was going to be a long red light. I could see the timer above the blinking green man indicating it was safe to walk in the direction I didn't want to go. It was going to be over a minute before I had the light again.

Breaking from my penny finding strategy, I decided to use my other "get somewhere" walking technique — following the path of least resistance. As long as I was moving south or west, I was good.

So, I took a hard right turn on a tree-lined residential street (no parking meters anywhere in sight) and cranked up my iPod. If I wasn't going to be finding pennies, I might as well get into the zone by listening to my favorite tunes!

I strolled down a series of similar streets for the next 15 minutes. Not a single store or a parking meter in sight. I'd all but stopped looking for change and was just enjoying the scenery as I walked.

But then, out of the corner of my eye, I caught a glimpse of something shiny. More specifically, it was SILVER and shiny!

Right there, in the middle of a place where it made no sense for it to be, lay a bright, shimmering DIME!

I didn't miss a beat as I hopped to the curb's edge to pick it up and slip it in my pocket. I couldn't help but smile as I hummed along to the song playing in my ears and continued walking toward my destination. A dime! And I hadn't expected it in the least! This might have turned out even better than my trip down 14th Street would have!

A short time later I arrived for my appointment and slipped quietly into the building. When I was done, I headed home with no real plan on how to get there. It would be a "path of least resistance" kind of walk.

I meandered my way from street to street. I found a penny here and another there. I even found another dime on a street full of parking meters and stores (can't go wrong there, I tell ya!).

I eventually made it back to 14th Street. At a bus stop just south of my condo I found eight pennies sprinkled in the road. Eight!

By the time I got back to my place, I'd amassed 36 cents from my round trip journey. My walk there had been almost peaceful. It gave me plenty of time to gather my thoughts, which was just what I'd needed for that particular appointment.

My trip back had been a mix of calm and cacophony. Quiet homes on one street and honking traffic on the next. DC is like that!

As I added my finds to the spreadsheet, I couldn't help but think about taking the road less traveled. There I'd been on a quiet, residential street where it made no sense to find any change. Maybe it was my highly trained eye (perfect circles don't occur in nature, remember?). Or maybe what I think I know about where to find pennies isn't right at all.

Whatever the case, I'd taken the road less traveled and it still got me not only where I needed to go, but where I WANTED to go. The appointment went fantastically well (it was a job interview, and I got the job) AND found a dime. I'd say I chose the right road!

The return road more traveled provided me with plenty of found money, too — sixteen pennies and another dime. Plus, it entertained me with new scenery and some great people watching, a much different experience than my quiet walk downtown, but just as enjoyable. And it got me where I WANTED to go!

Often times we fret about decisions to do one activity or another. Perhaps one path is "more traveled" and that's where you think you're supposed to go. But what does the other path look like? Is it more appealing to you?

After my little experiment of travelling down both the roads less and more traveled, I learned that each were equally wonderful for different reasons. Perhaps that is what ALL the decisions in our life are like.

Instead of worrying if you've made the right decision, just enjoy the decision you've made.

If you're on the road more traveled, there's likely to be lots of folks there to share the journey with you. Opportunities will abound, variety will be plentiful, and you're not likely to get bored. On this road, you will be one of many on the same path sharing similar experiences. If this is the kind of road that calls to you, TAKE IT!

But you might find yourself on the other road instead, the one less traveled and perhaps not so well marked. It might not be as well lit and you might be the only traveler at times, but you will see things that many others may never get to see. On this road, of many, you are one. You are carving your own unique experiences. If that is the kind of road that calls to you, TAKE THAT ONE!

As with my walk that day in DC, you will find that life gives you the tremendous opportunity to interchange the roads you travel, allowing you to choose how you want to live and how you want to get to your final destination at any given time. There may be periods in your life you choose to go on the fast route highway, sometimes running into traffic; and other times when you opt for the longer, scenic, and more isolated route where there is nothing but you, the road, and wide open spaces. The good news is whichever road you take, you are moving forward.

Lesson

There's a road out there for each of us and the good news is they're all connected! If you take a wrong turn or change your mind, you can always go back. Or better yet, just turn right at the next red light and see what the new road looks like.

Sometimes you just have to make the decision that whatever road you're on right now is the road you were meant to be on. And know, deep down, that somewhere along that road is a penny with your name on it! Or if you're lucky, a dime!

What are your 2 cents?

- Take a moment to reflect on what kind of roads you prefer.
- What's the best thing about the road you're on right now?
- When will you know you're ready to make a turn onto a new road?

Keepers

Why If You Look & Listen Closely, You Might See Some "Keepers" In YOUR Life

The other day I got a message on Facebook from a flight engineer I knew back in my CH-47 Chinook helicopter days.

Bobby was one of 38 people I deployed with to Kosovo. It was a small detachment of people for a Chinook unit (back then each company contained 16 aircraft and around 220 people), and the group became pretty tight-knit over the 12 months we trained and deployed.

I remembered Bobby as a hard worker, one of those guys who was really professional, always did his job, and never complained. He was on the quiet side until you got to know him, but once you did, he could throw out a comment that would just crack you up!

A few weeks prior to Bobby's message, someone had posted a picture on Facebook of the nine pilots that had been on that deployment. The picture was taken by the side of one of the helicopters.

It looked just like a picture the crew members had taken a week before. Crew members are the enlisted soldiers who specialize in the daily maintenance of the aircraft on the ground and in flight. They had organized themselves for a group photo and were pretty proud of how it turned out.

So were the pilots, who promptly stole the idea and did their own version of the photo.

The only difference was the crew members were none too happy the pilots couldn't come up with an idea of their own. Not enjoying the fact their idea had been ripped off, they decided to do something about it.

So, as the pilots stood smiling while their picture was being taken, three naked crew member behinds were being pressed up against the windows of the aircraft…right above the pilots' heads and clearly visible in the picture!

Not all of the pilots found the humor in this, but I thought it was a hoot! And it was even more of a hoot when it resurfaced on Facebook eight years later! Nothing reunites people like an embarrassing picture!

Within a few days, half a dozen people from that deployment resurfaced and commented on that photo. It was a great memory (people seem to find more humor when time passes) and we all got some good laughs out of reconnecting over it.

So many times I'd heard people say that of all the deployments they'd been on, THAT ONE was actually the most fun. Yes, we managed to enjoy ourselves, build great friendships, and have FUN on a deployment. Go figure.

So when Bobby's message appeared in my Inbox, I was sure it was going to be a comment about that picture (or, I was dreading, the other picture from that deployment where I was standing next to the Dallas Cowboy Cheerleaders looking completely disgruntled… please, don't let THAT one resurface!).

I was totally surprised when the message had nothing at all to do with pictures, deployments, or even the army. Instead, it was a few stories about pennies and change that Bobby thought might make good material for the book. What a great surprise!

Hey Leslie, I forgot to tell you, I have collected coins since I was little and I realized I have a few things that might be a good add for your material.

One I can think of right off the bat is the sound change makes. Over the years I would get change back and many times (as recent as two weeks ago) just by hearing the change clink in my hand I could tell there was a keeper there. I can only guess it's because I play piano, French horn, guitar, and other instruments. I'm good at playing by ear as well as reading music.

The situation is usually the same: I get change and I hear the coins. Every now and again I heard a different tone than what I consider normal. I look through them and sure enough, there is a "wheat back" penny or a silver dime or something else.

Once a guy kept putting a quarter in a coke machine and it kept coming back. He was getting pretty frustrated. I could hear the quarter as it clinked through and I asked him to see it. He handed me the quarter and I immediately knew it was a silver quarter. I gave him a regular quarter, he got his soda, and he thanked me while walking away. Coke machines today weigh the change and reject them if they are not the right weight. The silver change (1964 and older) is lighter in weight.

As I finished reading the message, I thought I would certainly be able to use his ideas. After all, how could I pass up a new take on change?!

I mulled it over for a few days and tried to think about how I could work it into a story. Was it about the sound change makes? I had said more than once to my friend Marissa, "I just heard a penny drop" while we waited in line at Target.

I could also hear other specific kinds of change (quarters are heavy, dimes are light, and nickels make more of a "ker-plunk"). Marissa often joked about dropping a handful of change and seeing if I could add it up by ear.

The unique sound some coins made intrigued me, but it was another word Bobby used that really won me over.

Keeper.

Those unique coins were keepers when he heard them jingling.

And as I mulled the message over and over, I thought, "Bobby is a keeper!" How cool is it to have someone I worked with eight years ago, and only see via the occasional interaction on Facebook, send me a personal story as inspiration for my book?

And like the "wheat back" pennies and silver quarter, we often have the people in our lives that stand out among the rest by saying or doing something to show us how special they are.

The question is, do we do what Bobby does and hold on to them, or do we let them slip through our fingers like any other piece of loose change?

I was inspired by this story to make a list of all the other keepers in my life. I already have a love for wheat pennies, but what else in my life belongs on the keeper list? Certainly I've got my fare share of people, places, and things I feel blessed to have in my life!

Once you get going on what my spiritual teacher, Abraham, likes to call a rampage of gratitude, it's tough to stop! Gratitude is one of those emotions that just feels so good! Below are a few things that made my "keepers" list. Read them, and then make your own list!

- My faux mink blanket (there's nothing better when it's below freezing outside)
- Starbucks gift cards for Christmas (then I don't feel guilty treating myself to a $6 latte)
- My mom (because she had to preview every chapter in this book as I wrote it)
- A good pair of flats (because walking 2 miles to work in 3" heels is ridiculous)
- My sister (for so many reasons…it's too hard to list just one!!)
- Marissa (my massaging, cooking, shoe-giving neighbor who also acts as my alarm clock on gym days)
- Hand written thank you cards (they're shockingly exciting to receive in the mail!)
- Snuggling with my cats (although they think my only job in life is to provide them with a lap, they too are fantastic when it's below freezing outside)

It feels great to take time and list the keepers in your life. It raises your focus from just seeing what you have to recognizing how fantastic it is! Then you can operate from a place of gratitude for all the great people, stuff, and places you're surrounded by.

And nothing feels better than being grateful for what you have. We often forget to recognize the abundance that surrounds us. It's easy to become so deafened by the everyday noise in our lives that we also tune out the sweet sound of the unique gifts…the "wheat backs"…that easily slip through our fingers if we don't take note!

Lesson

Make it a habit to take stock of the "keepers" in your life. Taking a little time to do that every day will shift your perspective from one of lacking to one of having.

When you take the time to make a list, or even a mental note of all the great things that surround you, you begin to see you probably have more things to list than space to list them. So go ahead, write a few down!

What are your 2 cents?

- What (or who) are your top five "keepers?"
- How can taking note of things you're thankful for become a daily habit (keep a journal, take pictures, make lists)?
- How can you show the human keepers on your list you're thankful they're in your life?

Playing
Why 4th Graders Have It Right
When It Comes To Work-Recess Balance

The same course I took that taught me to embrace and even celebrate failure, also taught me to play more when it comes to life.

I'd long been living under the assumption that there needed to be a work-me and a home-me (not to be confused with a "homey"). Sure, it was ok to be silly and laugh when I was being the home-me, but certainly that was not appropriate behavior in a work environment.

This class challenged that assumption when we did an exercise on the last day in which we had to sit still while our classmates told us what they loved and admired about our coaching, followed by what they wanted to see more of in our coaching.

To be clear, neither exercise was all that much fun. It was sort of uncomfortable to sit still, unable to respond, while people told me what they loved about me. Clearly, I was not so gracious at accepting compliments before this class!

But it was even more uncomfortable to sit still and listen to what people thought was lacking in my skill set without being able to defend myself. Talk about sitting on a hot seat!

When the comments started rolling in, they all sounded completely whacky to me. There were things I never expected to hear coming out of the mouths of people I worked with, such as:

- Be more of a nerd (could they not see what a nerd I was already? I track pennies on a spreadsheet!)
- Be a little less structured (wow…never heard THAT during my seven years in the military!)
- Be silly (like practical joke silly? I love that kind of silly!)
- Be more playful (playful?! I can do that at work? I've been trying NOT to be too playful!)

I couldn't believe these people were telling me to basically have more FUN in my work. I thought fun was something I could only have when I was being the home-me, not the work-me!

I spent the next several months playing with the idea of "fun in my work." What a concept! It turned out when I was silly, nerdy, playful, and a little less structured in my facilitation, training, or coaching, the results were better. All of the things that I had previously avoided doing turned out to be key factors in my successes!

I began to talk and think more about this whole idea. I even went back to my penny blog and pulled up some of my early entries.

Admittedly, I had stopped writing as much when more people started donating pennies and following the blog. I'd also changed the way I sent updates so people couldn't respond to the whole group. This was mostly due to the fact that my dad had a habit of hitting "reply all" and sharing his opinions about pennies via silly poetry and random thoughts.

Perhaps I had a bit of that fun-me vs. serious-me struggle as I tried to take these pennies and turn them into something bigger. I wanted to be taken seriously. Certainly, having too much fun wasn't the way to do that.

But when I went back and looked at some of the early blog posts — the ones influenced by the back and forth replies between the whole group — I realized that WAS what attracted people to the idea of picking up pennies. They enjoyed sharing the stories and excitement of their finds, such as, for example, when my dad sent out a poem via the "reply all" button. Those kinds of messages actually got responses. And then THOSE messages got responses. What's the obvious moral of this story? People liked to share and be silly!

Perhaps the witty back and forth banter was what made it so enjoyable in the first place. It was a way to be a part of something. To climb into a virtual sandbox like a 4th grader at recess and play with the other penny finders out there.

And so, in the spirit of uncovering some of that early fun, here is a blog post of poetry & prose that my Dad wrote, which was inspired by pennies and the people who find them. As you can see from the string of poems that ensued from my dedicated friends and penny finders, we clearly had fun with the dear old penny — and my dad — that day!

Date: October 25, 2007
From: Leslie's Dad
To: Leslie's Dad, Devoted Penny Finders
CC: Leslie
Subject: Poetry In Motion
Roses are red,
Violets are blue,
I found a dime today,
Did you?
I didn't say it was good poetry.
Jerry

Date: October 25, 2007
From: E
To: Leslie's Dad, Devoted Penny Finders
CC: Leslie
Subject: Poetry In Motion
Thanks for your bit of inspiration today – this has actually prompted me to try my hand at a bit of poetry myself.

Roses are red
Violets are blue
Some poems rhyme
But this one doesn't
Hmmmm . . . I suck at poetry.
E

Date: October 25, 2007
From: Rick
To: E, Leslie's Dad, Devoted Penny Finders
CC: Leslie
Subject: Poetry In Motion
hhhmmmmm.
Roses are Red,
Violets are Blue
If Lincoln were alive
He'd give you a high five.
oh well....I suck too.
Rick

Date: October 25, 2007
From: Julia
To: Rick, E, Leslie's Dad, Devoted Penny Finders
CC: Leslie
Subject: Poetry In Motion
I found a penny yesterday a-walking home from work.
Sir Lincoln's head was staring up, his tail smushed in the dirt.
His face was scratched up quite a bit but in all he seemed just fine,
for 'spite the cars and boots and grime, that penny kept its shine.
crosswalk of 7th and Maryland Ave, NE.
Julia

Who knew my dad, with his "reply all" habit, would inspire a string of poems by other penny finders? Not me! I had certainly warned him not to reply all, just like I had mentally warned myself not to have too much fun at work.

Thank goodness for the people in my class requesting more nerdyness. More silliness! More playfulness!

And thank goodness my dad ignored me and replied to everyone with his poems. The world didn't come to an end with a little bit of creative, childlike behavior, and I even got a good blog entry out of it!

Lesson

Get out there and play in the sandbox of life. Yes, even at work. Play inspires creativity. It inspires fresh ideas. It inspires others to want to jump in the sandbox with you!

I know what you're thinking, "Sure…it's easy for you to have fun. You pick up pennies and write about it for a living."

But at one point, I had stopped bringing fun to pennies because I was trying to be more "professional." Or at least what I THOUGHT it meant to be more professional.

Besides, it wasn't the penny finding that got me to loosen up. It was a professional workshop. I definitely didn't see THAT coming!

The next time you find yourself struggling to keep a stiff upper lip, when what you really want to do is say something ridiculous, try pushing the boundaries. Bringing a little of the "fun-you" to the world of your "work-you" just might be what's needed to get everyone else in the sandbox to create the next great idea.

What are your 2 cents?

- Where do you hold back the "fun-you" because you don't think it's appropriate?
- Where could being a little more playful in your life serve you well?
- Where in your life are you willing to try being a little more silly or playful to see what happens?

Grand Plans

Why You Might Enjoy The
Not So Grand Plans Just As Much

On day 32 of my 34-day writing challenge, my birthday was a mere three days away.

Instead of planning some big event that year, I let my birthday plans come to me. Sounds odd, but I decided just to see what turned up without me trying too hard.

I have to say… it went really well! I had a few pre-birthday events, something to look forward to ON my birthday (including a card labeled 'DO NOT OPEN UNTIL JANUARY 14, 2010' from my mommy), and even a post-birthday shin-dig. Not bad considering I didn't have to lift a finger!

Off the half a dozen pre-birthday events I had, each one was a lot of fun in its own way.

First, were my early birthday presents while visiting a friend out in Colorado, which included an ice fishing trip! Talk about a "cool gift!" And let's not overlook the fact I actually caught three fish my first time on the ice, a gift in and of itself. Even the fish conspired to make it a good birthday!

I returned home to DC to have an evening in with three girlfriends and the most fantastic meal, cooked from scratch, and certainly made with love! A bit on the impromptu side, but it ended up being a great mix of people and a night I won't forget (a picture of my birthday dessert appeared on Facebook before I left the table!).

The next night I met a close friend for drinks at a swanky speakeasy. There was one-on-one catching up, girl gab, tasty drinks, and a serving of rosemary-cheddar popcorn. Does it get any better?

After that it was an afternoon of crepes. A good friend who is also an amazingly good cook came over and made crepes in my kitchen. Eight other girls came too, each bringing incredibly yummy ingredients for the crepes AND a bottle of champagne. One girl even brought me a book about (what else) pennies! Let me count the ways this was the best day ever:

- Friends arrived bearing good food. Ok, screw the food. They brought good champagne!
- Someone else did the cooking in my kitchen
- Someone else cleaned up my kitchen
- We ate crepes until we couldn't move
- I got a new book about pennies
- I scored TONS of amazing leftovers (which promptly became my breakfast the next morning)

The next night I had dinner at a lovely neighborhood place. Creole food…delish! My date picked up the check. Boy is it good to be the birthday girl!

Next came dinner with two friends I hadn't seen in over a year on my actual birthday. Then it's off to a spa day with another girlfriend followed by a joint birthday happy hour someone else asked if she could plan for me. Score!

The interesting thing about all of these little celebrations was that they were each with different circles of friends. Each one has reminded me how lucky I am to know so many great people. Personally and professionally, I am surrounded by incredible people who I WANT to share my birthday with.

What's more, I want to share it with them in meaningful ways. A string of evenings with great conversation, good food, and lots of laughs sounds way more appealing to me than trying to come up with one big party that half the people probably wouldn't be able to attend do to scheduling difficulties.

I thought back to the way I felt when I found that first twenty dollar bill versus the little finds of change throughout the first year.

That twenty dollar bill represents the way I used to do things. Bigger. More. Grand! I remember previous birthdays with massive guest lists (sometimes full of people I felt I HAD to invite instead of just the ones I wanted to invite), kegs of beer (when I would have rather had champagne), and massive amounts of average food to feed the masses (instead of the smaller more savory dishes I really love).

After spending a few years picking pennies out of gutters, crawling around on metro bus floors for dimes, and scoring the occasional quarter at a toll booth, I find way more joy in the little things in my life.

Whether it be a quiet evening chatting with one friend, cooking a meal with my neighbor and then enjoying it with a few friends who can stop by on the way home from work, or stuffing myself silly with divinely delicious crepes, I no longer believe bigger is better. For all I care, you can keep your twenty dollar bill AND your big party if you'll leave me with my pennies and small gatherings.

Somewhere along the line, we've gotten the idea that everything needs to be a grand affair. Perhaps we believe things aren't worth having if they aren't accompanied by a big to-do.

But thinking back to my first year of pennies when all of my little finds added up to MORE than that first $20 bill, I realize the little things really do make us richer than the occasional grand affair.

So take stock of the small gestures. Reevaluate whether that "boring night in" is actually boring, or whether it is more accurately "intimate and cozy." And see if all your penny-sized celebrations aren't worth more than the overpriced affair that doesn't really suit you anyway.

Lesson

It's easy to get sucked into the mentality that bigger is better. With a constant stream of Hollywood images and news clips of "the haves" attending their lush galas, it's easy to feel like a simple happy hour with a few friends isn't all that exciting.

But ask yourself what you do when you go to a big gala. Do you mingle and hobnob with new people, or do you stick with the friends you came with and make fun of the other hobnobbers?!

If you're like most people, even when you do go to a big event, you end up spending your time with the people you came with. This should tell you that those oh-so-boring nights you think you're escaping aren't so bad after all!

What are your 2 cents?

- What are the little events in your life that make you feel richer?
- Who would you like to spend an uninterrupted evening with, just enjoying that person's company?
- What twist could you put on a random Tuesday evening to make it more memorable?

Following Your Heart
Why The Obvious Choice Isn't Always The RIGHT Choice

In 2010, after three and a half wonderful years in my Washington, DC condo, I decided it was time to sell it and move to Las Vegas. Contrary to popular belief, my plan was never to "bet it all on black" and see what happened.

My parents had been living in Las Vegas for about eight years and right as I was thinking about moving, the condo they'd been renting to a friend became available. The cost of living was about a third of what it was in DC. Not to mention, my mom was enticing me to move by promising me free labor as a part-time employee three days a week. All things considered, it was a great way to reduce my cost of living (and therefore the amount of time I had to spend working), which would allow me more time to focus on the two projects I loved most, one of which was The Penny Project!

Despite my desire to grow The Penny Project, the decision to sell my place in Washington, DC was not an easy one. I had what I believed was the city's best condo. It was in an area conveniently located to shopping, dining and metro access, AND it had a private patio that my very first house guest said "didn't make sense." That's because no one in DC has a 600 square foot private patio. In fact, most studio apartments in DC don't even have 600 square feet of living space. There are members of Congress that would've been jealous if they'd seen my outdoor space!

But as good as it was I knew it was time to let it go in favor of something better...following my heart.

I wasn't worried about the logistics of the sale because I knew the realtor I was going to use. He sold me the condo and was a barrel of fun to work with. If I was going to sell my lovely place, HE was my guy!

Considering myself a somewhat wise and learned person (or at least not a dumb one), I thought it would be good to get more than one perspective on the sale of my condo. My sister's friend Dina was a realtor and had come to my place for a party not long after I moved in. She told my sister, "I LOVE Leslie's place — it's market ready NOW!! If she ever wants to sell, tell her I would love to be her realtor!"

Flattery gets you everywhere. And so, three years later, with her complimentary words still in mind, I contacted Dina for a "second opinion."

Turns out she was available before the other guy, so she became my FIRST opinion.

From the moment she walked in the door, everything she said was positive. She loved the colors, the décor, and of course, the patio. She was certain that would make it a hot commodity, even in the luke-warm real estate market we were experiencing at the time. She said I didn't need to change a thing and that we could have the unit on the market in just a few weeks. She offered a range of listing prices I was happy with and showed me her plan to market and sell the unit.

All good information, but really just a place holder until my guy showed up the next day. Except that when my guy DID show up, everything began to unravel from the moment he walked in the door.

At the time, the first thing visitors saw as they entered my unit was the penny wall. A collection of framed art, notes from penny finders, and even a dinner plate sized penny paying homage to my love for found money. As soon as my realtor saw this he said, "This will have to come down — entirely too personal."

Gulp!

I knew he was good at what he did — he was one of the best. But Dina hadn't thought it was a problem and actually kind of liked it. Guess it was a good thing HE was my guy to keep me from leaving up something that would keep my place from selling. Right?

Well, as the conversation unfolded there were lots of other things he thought needed to change. The way the curtains were hung and touch-up paint in the hallway — maybe even a new color. But we could hire people to do that. And he definitely wouldn't put it on the market until after Labor Day. Since we were talking in July, the date seemed a bit farther off than I had hoped.

Again, I thought back to my conversation with Dina who'd thought we could put it on the market right away. Her theory was that it was a great unit and unlike anything else on the market. Yes, July and August were typically slower months, but she was not concerned that this would affect the sale of my condo.

But THIS was my guy...not Dina. Surely she was mistaken and the advice he was giving me was correct.

Then came the issue. The one that made me realize perhaps this wasn't going to be the slam dunk I had hoped for — it was time to talk about pricing. When he told me where he thought we should price the unit, it was not just a little bit lower than what Dina recommended. It was like they were pricing two different homes. I was baffled how they could come up with pricing ranges that didn't even cross each other. His high end was lower than her low end.

I was starting to think I was in serious trouble.

On the one hand I had "my guy." Except, for being "my guy," it seemed he didn't think the unit looked all that good, didn't believe we could sell it right now, and wasn't sure we should price it in a range where I'd even make my money back, let alone walk away with a profit.

Then there was Dina, the back-up realtor. She was telling me the unit looked amazing, that I didn't need to change a thing (even the penny wall could stay), that we could list it as soon as I was ready, and was willing to price it in a range that would allow me to walk away with a nice profit (and pretty certain we'd get an offer at that price).

It's funny how sometimes we think we know EXACTLY what we want, but when we see it next to something else that wasn't even really an option, it doesn't look so good after all.

What seemed like a slam dunk choice turned out to be a no brainer in the complete opposite direction. I hadn't expected it, but I chose Dina to sell my place. The funny thing was that neither she nor "my guy" expected my decision, either. It was a collective surprise to all of us, but definitely the right decision.

And so to market we went, penny wall and all.

The first open house was two days after the property was listed. I vacated the premises and waited for the all-clear signal from Dina after the event was over. She said there had been lots of traffic and some legitimate interest. She said above all else, she wished we could sell homes based on the energy match of the buyer and seller because there had been a couple looking at the house in which the woman also picked up found money! What were the odds?

It was an interesting thought, but I knew it wasn't a way to pick a buyer, so I just waited to see if any offers came in.

A day went by. Then two. Then three. Four. Nothing.

By Friday, five days after the open house, I was talking to some friends and worried that perhaps I had priced it too high. Maybe Dina and I had been over-confident and would have to end up lowering the price if we didn't get any offers within the next week. One of them suggested putting some positive thoughts in my mind by writing myself a check for a full price offer.

I loved the idea. I'm all about attracting things you want by focusing on the positive and figured the message to the Universe would be that I believed a full price offer was coming my way. So I grabbed my checkbook, wrote the check for the full price, and then put that day's date on it with three arrows pointing to it. If I was going to manifest a full price offer, I might as well not drag it out!

I figured I'd done all I could on my end and opted to spend the rest of the afternoon at the pool with a friend. I grabbed a novel, put my phone on silent, and sunk into a lounge chair to forget my real estate woes.

After we'd had our fill of sun and lounging, we packed up to head home. I quickly turned my phone back to its normal ring setting and saw I had a voicemail message. It was from Dina. I dialed in wondering what news she had for me.

Whilst I had been lounging at the pool, we had received not one… not two…but THREE full price offers for the condo! Three arrows to the day's date on my check…three offers. Coincidence? Methinks not.

Dina said the paperwork would be ready the next morning and that she'd swing by the house to go over it with me. When she arrived, we sat down at the dining room table to review the offers. "This is going to be hard," she said.

Hard? We had three full-price offers…what could be so difficult?!

First, she told me about an offer that could easily be labeled "the offer" from a couple who had 20% to put down and was willing to pay full price. No request for help with closing costs. Cha-ching! Did I even need to hear about the other offers? This sounded nearly perfect!

The second offer, it turned out, was from the couple she loved from the open house — the one with the woman who also picked up found money. And although it was a full price offer, they were asking for closing help — $10,000 of closing help. That would mean $10,000 less in my pocket at the end of the day.

OK, I could see why she thought this was going to be difficult. But really, in all honesty, this was a business decision. Didn't it just make sense to go with the best offer?

Oh, but wait…she hadn't told me about the letter.

The letter?

Yes, the letter. The penny couple (as they came to be called) had written a letter about why they thought this was the perfect new home for them, and about our shared love for pennies. It was straight from the heart. Just like their offer, they were giving all they had. There was no room for more.

The 20% down offer was amazing. Nothing wrong with it and certainly another one of those slam dunk situations.

But it was also an offer from the head with contingencies and escalation clauses. It just didn't feel the same as the offer that came with the letter, which really felt like it was from the heart. That couple KNEW this was their home. It was a place their dog Stella and "Piggy" (the 30+ pound piggy bank with all the found money from the last six years) would be happy to call home.

I had some thinking to do.

But not really.

Just like I'd followed my gut about picking Dina even though I had been sure "my guy" was the right realtor, I knew I had to follow my gut — or more accurately in this case, my heart — and bypass "the offer" for what I knew was the right decision for me.

I called Dina and asked if they'd be willing to split the difference by going $5,000 over the asking price so we'd essentially be splitting the closing costs down the middle. So began the game of telephone from me to my realtor to their realtor to them, and then back again to finally say "yes." They would indeed accept my counter offer and go over the asking price to close the deal.

My favorite poem, you may remember, has always been "The Road Less Traveled" by Robert Frost. I've always been one to take that road and this situation was no different.

I'm sure most people would have taken the offer that netted the most. But that was not my road.

My road led to eventually meeting the couple that bought my condo. It led to hearing how when they saw the penny wall they KNEW that was their home. It led to my friend Laura making a film about The Penny Project that included an interview with me and my buyers about our experiences on each side of that transaction. And it led to knowing that the final chapter in my DC penny story was really just a new beginning, a new beginning for them in my condo and a new beginning for me in Las Vegas. No sad endings for the road not taken, only happy memories of the road we chose and where it led us.

Lesson

As someone who's well versed on the road less taken, I speak from experience when I say that it's an amazing road. Yes, it can be exhausting. And yes, sometimes it doesn't turn out at all like you think it will. So be open to things going in the complete opposite direction than you had planned. If you decide to venture down an unbeaten path, there's nothing like the feeling of being the first to see what it has to offer!

You can absolutely play it safe and take the road others have taken if that's what works for you. Slam dunks and sure things are great when they work in your favor. But sometimes, to find out which decision are right for YOU, you have to listen to your own inner voice instead of the voices of those around you.

Learn to trust your instincts and pick YOUR road, not the one everyone else thinks you should take. If I was on the road "most taken", I'd probably still be trying to sell my condo in DC. I'd have a routine desk job instead of living my passion. Or perhaps I'd be one chapter short for this book because some couple who happened to have a 20% down payment bought my place.

What are your 2 cents?

- Where do you listen to everyone else when your heart is telling you something different? What are the results of following them versus your own heart?
- What opportunities might you gain by letting go of the way you KNOW things are supposed to turn out and being open to other possibilities?
- How would you fill out a blank check in your life? To whom? For what? When?

My 34¢ On Letting Go
Why Changing The Original Plan
Might Just Save Your Sanity

Dear Lord, there really IS a light at the end of the proverbial tunnel! You may have noticed when you started this chapter that there was a slight deviation from the standard formula that starts every other chapter. While all the other chapters have been titled "My 2¢ on X-Subject,"THIS chapter has 34¢ worth of advice. Either this advice is a whole lot more valuable or something weird is going on.

My original intention when I set out to write the book was to have 50 chapters each with "My 2¢" on something, thereby leaving readers with a dollar's worth of advice. That was a great idea when I started writing. It was not such a great idea, however, when I realized I only had about 30 stories on my list of penny-lessons-learned. Nor when I realized just how much time it took to write one chapter.

It also didn't help that my whole goal of "I want to write this in 34 days... but not just any 34 days...the LAST 34 days I'm 34!"fell smack dab over Christmas, New Year's, and a 10-day trip to Colorado to visit friends.

Wow...talk about a bad plan!

But despite it all, I was compelled to write and got in a pretty good rhythm once I got going. So I decided just to write and see what happened.

About 20 chapters into the book, I called my mom in a bit of distress and said I wasn't sure I was going to be able to finish 50 chapters in 34 days. Although some chapters came quite easily, others were more challenging and left me wondering how I could maintain my original pace.

She said, "Look...the idea of writing 50 chapters led you to the 'My 2¢' idea, which you love and we all think is cute. But what if you let go that there has to be a dollar's worth of advice? What if you just had, say, 60 cents worth?"

I wasn't loving it. Who buys a book called "60 Cents Worth of Advice on Life"? I told her as much while we mulled it over.

"Ok, fine," she continued, not the least bit dissuaded by the fact I wasn't buying her less-than-a-dollar idea, "What if you make the last chapter more than two cents? You write as many chapters as you have ideas and then when you see what you've got, you make the last chapter 'My 38¢ on Whatever.' You can write the last chapter about how sometimes you have to be adaptable and let go of the original plan."

I had to chuckle. The idea reminded me of my cow summer at West Point (how cruel is it that I had to call myself a cow instead of a junior like other college kids my age — talk about an esteem buster!).

That summer I had been a squad leader for Beast Barracks, the cadet equivalent of basic training. My job was to whip the new class of sniveling, whining civilians into uniform-wearing, hard charging cadets. In my case, this meant being the ma'am/sir police.

As a female cadet, I got called 'sir' more times that summer than any woman ever should. A cow called sir...either an intriguing title for my next book or the makings of a somewhat depressed 20-something year old who was feeling less than feminine.

Fortunately, my roommate Kristen and I had come up with an amusing way to deal with the repeated 'sir' offenders we encountered that summer. Each time a new cadet called either one of us sir, we had him or her (yes, the girls did it to us, too) make us a list of ten differences between men and women.

The smart ones gave us lists that said things like, "Women are funnier than men." No argument there. We'd skim the rest and let the offender go.

Others wanted to be tough guys and put stuff like "Men are stronger than women." Of course these lists bared much greater scrutiny and discussion. How would men fare in child birth? Why don't I kick you in the groin and we see how strong you are then?

But my favorite list that summer came from a guy who was either blind, a moron, or both. He called Kristen and I 'sir' a combined total of something like 12 times. He could no sooner write a list than he'd be doing it again. It was brutal.

We told him he clearly needed more than just our basic remedial training. We ordered him to report to us the next morning with a list of 100 differences between men and women. Surely after completing such an exercise, he would not want to make the same mistake again.

The next morning he delivered a thick envelope with several hand-written pages of differences between men and women. His list ranged from the obvious to the anatomical and everything in between. But what really caught my attention was that somewhere way down on the list, we found the following:

64) Men are generally taller than women.

65) Women can give birth.

79) Men can't count.

Two words flashed through my mind. Pure genius.

Not only had this kid done his best to give us a good list, but he'd also used humor and taken a risk by skipping #66-78. Pretty clever.

As that memory came back to me while my mom was telling me to let go a little and just fudge the numbers on that last chapter, I knew she was right.

I'm sure some people will buy this book and get to chapter 34 to feel they've been bamboozled. But the rest of you will just smile, read this chapter and know that sometimes in life, you have to let go, take a risk, and keep a good sense of humor about it all.

So that's the approach I took. After that conversation, I just wrote the stories I had to write. Some were easy, others were a bit more difficult, but as I worked my way down the list I'd made (and added a few thanks to the inspiration of friends along the way), I knew wherever I stopped would be the right place.

When I was within just a few chapters of being done, a friend pointed out to me that there was something numerologically significant about the number 34. I was 34, I'd finish writing in 34 days, and so why not do 34 chapters? I think the idea was that 3+4=7 and with all those 34's I'd create a triple 7. Nice stroke of luck if I wanted it!

I decided that 34 was the new "right" number and that the added bit of structure at the end would be a good way to help me sprint across the finish line instead of limp across it!

I thought back to that conversation with my mom and started doing the math in my head. If I do 33 chapters at 2¢ each then I'd need… wait, are you serious?! I'd need 34¢ to make my dollar. It was too perfect to pass up.

So here it is. The 34th and final chapter in a book full of lessons I've learned by picking up pennies. I guess I actually had to start writing about them to fully grasp this last lesson, but it just might be one of the most important.

We live in a pretty goal oriented society. While I'm not saying to stop setting goals, I AM saying to be a little more forgiving of yourself when you see the original goal may not suit your needs anymore.

My mom is a big proponent of finishing what you start, so I grew up with the engrained belief that you shouldn't abandon goals when they get too hard or when you've grown bored with them. Believe me, if that was my outlook, I'd have bailed on this project back in chapter 13 when I had a serious case of sophomore slump!

In a nutshell, my point is that life changes very quickly, which invariably leads to setting goals in uncharted territory. So one of the best gifts we can give ourselves is the permission to alter, change, or make a mess of our original goals to help them suit the current conditions.

I let go of a perfectly round number of 2¢-chapters that would've added up to a dollar's worth of advice in favor of writing the best stories possible, topped off with one 34¢-lesson at the end. In the midst of my writing, I realized there's no hard, fast guideline about how many chapters a book needs to have.

Just because you change a goal, doesn't mean you're not meeting it. Letting go and doing the best writing I could do led to a book I am extremely proud of.

34 chapters DOES a book make. Or at least, it makes THIS book!

Lesson

Goals are important. They are what help us stretch ourselves and move forward in this journey we call life. But it's important to use them as a tool for growth and not become a slave to them just because they've been set.

This is especially true when you're setting goals in new territory! Are you running your first marathon? Just because Oprah did it in 4.5 hours doesn't mean it's the right goal for you. Start training and see what feels like a realistic (or optimistic) goal for you based on YOUR abilities — not on Oprah's!

In the end, you may find that letting go allows you to reshape the goal into something better than what it originally started out to be. Or you may not. Either way, there's a power in letting go that sometimes provides just the right motivation for achieving your goal(s).

So let go of that strangle hold you have on an old, unrealistic goal. Open your hand and let the new, achievable goal breath freely. One of my favorite quotes is "When your hand is open to give, it's open to receive."

And maybe then you'll receive the motivation you seek.

What are your 2 cents?

- What goal(s) do you need to let go of or reshape?
- How might your "new" goal(s) reinvigorate you?
- Next time you set a goal, how can you make a plan to reevaluate the goal itself (not just your progress) as the journey unfolds? You're Invited

An Invitation
To Join The Penny Finding Fun

Inspired by what you've read? Have your own ideas about
pennies, everyday miracles, or life lessons from the ordinary?
We'd love to hear about YOUR penny perspectives!!
Come visit us at *www.pennyperspectives.com* to share your
stories, pictures, thoughts, & comments.
Joy is waiting for you...will you join it?

CPSIA information can be obtained at www.ICGtesting.com
Printed in the USA
BVOW010656011212

307007BV00005B/35/P